PROJECT MANAGEMENT TECHNIQUES

PROJECT MANAGEMENT TECHNIQUES

Alfred O. Awani

a petrocelli
book
new york / princeton

Copyright © 1983 Petrocelli Books, Inc.
All rights reserved.

Designed by Diane L. Backes
Typesetting by Backes Graphics

Printed in the United States of America
1 2 3 4 5 6 7 8 9 10

Library of Congress Cataloging in Publication Data

Awani, Alfred O.
  Project management techniques.

  Bibliography: p.
  Includes index.
  1. Industrial project management. I. Title.
T56.8.A95   1983   658.4'04   83-2210
ISBN 0-89433-197-3

CONTENTS

PREFACE

The subject of project management which is concerned with planning, scheduling, and controlling of nonroutine activities within certain time and resource constraints includes a wide range of topics. Hundreds of articles and papers and several books have appeared relating to network planning and critical path analysis. Network planning, scheduling, and control systems offer tremendous potential for future exploitation. All their past and present uses build a solid foundation for radical innovation in project management concepts.

This book is not intended as an exhaustive treatise. Instead its purpose is introductory, aimed at serving two types of readers: first, the beginning or practicing project manager in the field who is not thoroughly familiar with modern techniques of network analysis, and second, those senior or graduate students who elect to study the subject of project management and related questions.

The book focuses on basics and presents the essentials in a simple, straightforward manner, so that it can be used as an individual guide to planning, scheduling, and controlling techniques in project management.

Chapters 1 through 8 cover the concepts and techniques of project management. Emphasis is placed on a systematic treatment of the subject. The general tone for this text is to address the need for procedures which allow projection of the possible future stages of a project through to completion. Chapter 9 addresses the subject of project proposals—this is considered important, since it serves as a framework for developing a detail plan and schedule to be used in carrying out a project. In chapter 10, discussion focuses on project personnel selection; the author believes that one of the first and most important ingredients of any successful project is the selection of the right project manager, since each project has a unique set of circumstances that tend to demand a unique set of qualifications in its manager.

Chapter 11 deals with various types of contracts likely to be selected by a customer as the most feasible for a contemplated procurement. Chapter 12 presents a television tower and building project. Chapter 13 follows this up by treating a project management simulation; this device allows the project manager or student to participate in a dynamic interactive way, whereby the student plans the project prior to its beginning and then he or she directs the project as it unfolds in response to a series of unpredictable and randomly introduced variables that cause the project situation to change as time progresses. The author believes that this procedure would allow the student the opportunity to assume the role of the project manager in making decisions throughout the duration of the project, and will also provide the student with an in-depth examination of the concepts and techniques discussed in the text.

Chapter 14 presents various case studies, which can be used as class projects. Appendix A addresses the normal distribution and illustrates the significance of the mean of standard deviation. Appendix B explains the activity-on-arrow system of networking and a procedure for converting from activity-on-node system (which is used in the text) to activity-on-arrow system. Appendix C discusses the event-oriented systems, and comparision is made with the activity-on-node and activity-on-arrow systems. Appendix D presents a listing of table of random numbers. Finally, Appendix E stresses a computer method.

Emphasis throughout the text is on questions, e.g., planning, scheduling and control techniques, which can be described by project evaluation and review technique and critical path method. The author, with some regrets, has not heavily emphasized certain topics to which a decided emphasis has been given in the literature; this has been largely the result of the nature of his own particular experience rather than an intention to slight such material.

The intent of the author has been as, a minimum goal, to present a resumé of representative management practices in the project management field.

This text is dedicated to Denise for her encouragement, patience and lost weekends, and to my parents, sisters, and nephew Leo for their inspiration.

Alfred O. Awani
San Jose, California

NOMENCLATURE

a	Optimistic time
A-O-A	Activity-on-Arrows
A-O-N	Activity-on-Nodes
b	Pessimistic time
C_c	Crashed activity cost
C_D	Drag Coefficent
C_n	Normal activity cost
C.O	Crane Operator
CPM	Critical Path Method
CUMUL.	Cumulative
d_f	Flap deflection
DPC	Direct Project Cost
EF	Earliest Finish Time
ES	Earliest Start Time
FF	Free Float
IPC	Indirect Project Cost
K	Crashing cost for each activity
LF	Latest Finish Time
LS	Latest Start Time
m	Most probable time
M	Maximum possible activity time reduction due to crashing

PERT	Project Evaluation and Review Technique
Prob.	Probability
R & D	Research and Development
SD	Standard Deviation
t	Activity completion time
T	Project Completion Time
τ	Normal activity time
τ'	Crash activity time
TF	Total Float
TV	Television
V	Project time variance
v	Variance of the activity time

Chapter

1

INTRODUCTION TO
PROJECT MANAGEMENT

Network-based procedures of PERT (Program Evaluation and Review Technique) and CPM (Critical Path Method) are well known and widely used to assist managers in planning and controlling both large and small projects of all types (construction, research, development projects, and many others).

Many managerial problems in the areas of project scheduling and control have been solved successfully with the aid of network models and network analysis techniques. Effective planning and scheduling are absolutely essential to the success of these types of activities.

The words "planning" and scheduling" are common to completely different problems. For many years considerable operations research activity has been spent in the area of "production scheduling." In general, the techniques developed for this area are directed toward solving for sequences that minimize man or machine idle time subject to constraints. In most cases this effort has been primarily concerned with repetitive activities generally in continuous-flow production situations. Only recently has any significant effort been devoted to the study of the planning and scheduling problems of the class of operations known as projects or one-time operations.

The need for procedures which allow projection of the possible future stages of a project through to completion led to the adoption of the network as a desirable means of depicting the elements of a project and the relationships among them. This network idea is the basis of all critical

1

path analysis schemes and is used to depict a project plan. Much of the early success of PERT/CPM was based on the explicitness of the project plan, this explicitness being essential to the construction of a network. Being explicit about what was to take place at some later time was a new experience for many. Improved communications among those concerned with a given project were common results of networking the project plan.

Among the many operations that may be classed as projects are heavy and light construction, facilities maintenance, shipbuilding, the research and development phases of military weapon systems acquisitions, indeed any set of activities requiring a one-time oriented coordination of men, equipment, and materials. These operations tend to have several things in common, such as:

1. The end products of each operation are few in number.

2. Each operation is composed of a large number of serial and parallel jobs.

3. All of these jobs are directed toward a common objective.

4. A significant amount of uncertainty exists regarding the exact manner in which the objective is to be accomplished, how long it will take and how much it will cost. The degree of uncertainty with which each operation is perceived will vary depending on such factors as the state of the technology employed and the number of times similar operations have been performed in the past.

5. Different jobs are done by different organizations which have difficulty communicating with each other.

Planning and scheduling have always played an important role in project-type operations. However, most earlier planning systems had deficiencies resulting from the use of techniques which were inadequate for dealing with complex projects. Generally, the several groups concerned with the work did their own planning and scheduling. Since much of this was independent, the results often reflected a lack of coordination in carrying out the work. In addition, it is traditional in project operations to develop detailed schedules from gross estimates of total requirements and achievements based on past experience. Plans and schedules based on this data tend to consider all the pertinent factors bearing on the problem at one time.

The lack of adequate tools and techniques has been primarily responsible for these conditions. Most of the traditional scheduling techniques are based on the Gantt or bar chart which has been in common use for over 50 years. Although it is still a valuable tool, its use is limited in the scheduling of large-scale operations. In particular, the bar chart fails to delineate the complex interactions and precedence relationships which exist among the project activities. The milestone system used extensively by the military and industry for the management of major projects prior to the advent of PERT was an important link in the evolution from the Gantt chart to the network concept. Milestones are key events or points in time which can be uniquely identified when reached as the project progresses. The milestone system provides a sequential list of the various tasks to be accomplished in the project. This innovation was important because it emphasized the functional elements of the program, reflecting what is now the project work-time breakdown or product indenture structure. This system increased awareness, if not the effective display, of the interdependencies between tasks.

While the milestone system has the limitation that the relationship between milestones is not established, it is still widely used usually as an adjunct to the network system. Milestones are merely listed in a chronological sequence and are not related in a logical sequence of work required to accomplish them. Therefore, the essential interrelationships cannot be displayed. The system was an important early recognition of the need for awareness and discipline at lower management levels and forces outcome-oriented planning of all the segments of the projects.

Network planning, scheduling, and control systems offer tremendous potential for future exploitation. All their past and present uses build a solid foundation for radical innovation in project management concepts. The literature is already filled with examples of vastly improved planning by applying trade-off or optimization techniques to time, dollars, and labor. However, the ability to allocate resources over multiple projects means that it is possible to develop a total corporate planning system.

Future projections with network systems are no longer theoretical topics, and they offer significant long-range benefits to business management. The relationship of the network system to the management function and the outlook for further development of the system, perhaps even leading to a valid general system theory for the management of human enterprises, is extremely promising.

SUCCESSFUL IMPLEMENTATION

A decision by an organization to initiate a critical path scheduling system usually requires some form of training for the firm's personnel and for representatives of cooperating companies. Training may take the form of a brief indoctrination session, a detailed short course, or on-the-job training. Unquestionably, the detailed short course followed by a formal on-the-job training program best ensures success for the new system.

ROLE OF NETWORKS IN A PROJECT MANAGEMENT SYSTEM

The network models are means of describing a particular project plan in a manner such that evaluation is not only possible but is in fact a logical extension of the model. A given model of this basic type will describe *one* alternative project plan. Other models will be required if other alternatives are to be examined.

The network concept involves the graphical representation of activities and their precedence requirements. Activities are elements of the project which represent logical subdivisions of the work to be done. If you considered preparing breakfast as a project, pouring a cup of coffee could be an activity. The level of detail used depends upon the degree of control desired. As an extreme example, if control is desired only on the start of a project, the entire project may be described as a single activity. Precedence requirements indicate which activities must be completed before a given activity can proceed. The network may be thought of as indicating the time flow of work involved in the project. The network is *not* a schedule. It is not necessary to know the estimated time duration of activities before networking the project. In fact, this property makes it possible to separate the network modeling process from all other aspects of the planning phase. The likelihood that innovative and effective plans will be produced is improved by the use of the time-free networking process.

The basic purpose of the network is to provide a comprehensive picture of the precedence relationships existing among activities. Precedences are determined by comparing the environments created by the completion of an individual activity in the project with the environment necessary for the start of the succeeding individual activities. Resource availability and customary practice are not to be considered as creating prece-dence relationships. Both of these factors can be considered later during the scheduling phase, but inclusion in the planning phase may preclude the possibility of eventually arriving at the best schedule.

There are two basic systems of networking currently in use. The arrow diagramming, or activities-on-arrows (A-O-A) system, is more widely used, but the precedence diagramming, or activity-on-nodes (A-O-N) system, is growing in popularity and has significant advantages. *The A-O-N prece-dence diagramming system is used throughout this text.* The activities-on-arrows (A-O-A) system is explained in Appendix B and a procedure for converting from A-O-N to A-O-A is given.

REFERENCES

Awani, Alfred O., and Schweikhard, W.G. *Planning, Scheduling and Controlling Techniques in Engineering Project Management* (unpublished). University of Kansas, May 1980.

Buchan, Russell J., and Davis, Gordon J. *Project Control Through Network Analy-sis and Synthesis.* Atlanta: DDR International, 1976.

Chapter
2
COMPONENTS OF PROJECT MANAGEMENT

Project management is concerned with planning, scheduling, and controlling nonroutine activities within certain time and resource constraints. It may be broadly described as making and enforcing the necessary decision as to what, how, who, when, and where. Two roles are involved in these decisions. One of these is that of the project manager. In tracing the managerial chain of command up from the implementation level, the first position which has the authority to give an implementable answer to all the above questions is the project manager. He has the authority over and responsibility for the conduct of the project.

Although project management ideas are applied under a variety of different titles in different organizations, there are a number of salient factors which characterize most applicants:

1. The project manager operates independently of the organization's normal chain of command—a "horizontal hierarchy" comes into being, reflecting an amalgamation of interfunctional resources directed toward a specific goal having time, cost, and technical performance parameters.

2. The project manager negotiates directly for support from functional elements; normal line and staff relationships give way to a "web of relationships" directed to the beginning and completion of specific undertakings within the organization.

7

3. While the role of the project manager may vary widely from one of a coordinating nature to "general manager" function, he or she is the single focal point of contact for bringing together organizational effort toward a single project objective.

4. The organizational life of the project tends to be finite in nature. A particular project ends but will be replaced by another which involves a different product mix, advanced technology, or slightly different objectives. In the ongoing and healthy organization there will be a continuous flow of projects which represent the basic building blocks of the organization's business.

5. A deliberate conflict exists between the project and the functional purposes of the organization. The functional elements are charged with maintaining a pool of resources to support the organizational effort, whereas the project is directed to delivering a product or service on time, within budget, and in satisfaction of the technical performance requirements. Open hostility can break out between the project manager and functional department heads over the competition for the time and talent of department personnel.

6. Each project involves more than one subdivision of the organization; usually the project has companywide application.

7. Projects can originate from anywhere in the company. Projects having as their purpose the application of technology will usually originate on the research and development (R & D) side of the house; those primarily of a marketing nature (such as a product manager application) will emerge in marketing.

8. The project cannot be carried out totally within one division or functional element.

9. An individual is needed to assume total responsibility and accountability for project success (or failure).

The second project management role is that of the project management systems engineer. This individual occupies an advisory position to the project manager(or project managers) and will be referred to here as the consultant. This person has the responsibility for obtaining and processing basic project information and presenting to the project manager the appropriate data, in the most effective format, at the best time, so that the best possible decisions can be made by the project manager. The consultant should continually ask the question why to all the other questions and document the answer for all decisions that are made.

Neither the project manager nor the consultant needs to be expert in the other's specialty, but some basic cross-education should be achieved early in the project planning stage of the project management process. Frequently, on small- to moderate-sized projects the project manager fills both roles.

A project management system should become operational with the selection of individuals to fill the two roles mentioned above. The project manager will then add members to the project organization as their talents become needed. These needs will develop as the project management system carries out its various functions, which are to:

1. *Obtain detailed specifications of project objectives.* Too often, projects are started without consensus among those involved as to what the end product is to be. Haziness as to project objectives will be reflected in ambiguous, vague, or internally incompatible project plans.

2. *Obtain a specific statement of management objectives.* Until the management objectives are known, no judgment can be made about a suggested project plan.

3. *Determine what major alternative approaches to carrying out the project exist.* Rarely is there only one method or strategy that will achieve the project objectives. Yet many project managers adopt the first feasible plan that comes to mind. Time spent early in the planning stage searching for alternatives is usually an excellent investment.

4. *Estimate the results anticipated from each of the more promising alternatives.* The alternatives to be compared must be made explicit in terms of their time, cost, and resource requirements. This explicitness must be sufficient to distinguish the differences in tactics involved in the alternatives.

5. *Evaluate the results expected from the best alternative.* The quantifiable and nonquantifiable factors are combined in an overall

judgment as to which is the "best" alternative. This alternative is then evaluated in terms of the management objectives previously determined.

6. *Decide whether or not further planning is required.* If the plan does not gain management approval, either the plan, or the management objectives, or both must be changed. Frequently the true management objectives can be determined only after a plan is prepared, presented, and reviewed.

7. *Produce and distribute the information necessary to convey the plan and schedule to the users.* The concepts and conversations of the planners during the planning process are not available to the normal operating personnel unless written down. Care must be taken to ensure that the documents issued convey a full and clear description of the project plan and schedule.

8. *Implement the plan and schedule selected by management.* The system hinges on the people who convert the plans into reality. Good people frequently need a nudge to get them moving on the right activity. Competent and informed direct supervision is one of the keys to successful implementation.

9. *Periodically review the status of the project with respect to the management objectives.* This updating should review the extent of implementation and see if the project is still expected to meet the project and management objectives originally set up for it. If not, a review of management objectives and alternative plans is again in order so that an acceptable approach to the remainder of the project is in effect.

After the periodical review of the status of the project with respect to management objectives (evaluation phase), project management may sometimes require changes in the project plan, in the basic resources assigned to the project, or even in the basic project concept and objectives. Encountering this need for change is not a reason for despair or inaction. Projects are set up to cope with situations of uncertainty and complexity. Project management is as much concerned with keeping the project moving after it is started as it is with the initial planning. Reprogramming is the term used here to designate this part of the project management component.

REPROGRAMMING*

Reprogramming proceeds directly out of the evaluation phase in which accomplishments to date and estimated future progress are compared with project plans and directives. Variances are analyzed during the evaluation *activity to determine* their magnitude and causes. The reprogramming can take place to correct them.

A first approach to correcting variances may be to call for better performance on the part of an executing department, perhaps bringing this about by eliminating misunderstandings concerning what is desired, or it may be to ensure the availability of intended information and resources. This is simply a matter of clarifying direction and improving performance so that the original plan can be followed.

If it is simply not possible to carry out the details of the original plan, then the subplans must be made to conform to the original plan. If there is a schedule problem in a department, it may be permitted to extend its schedule by reprogramming the downstream work that depends on its output. Or if it is a budgetary problem, additional budget may be provided out of reserves or by transferring funds from some other less critical path of the project. In these solutions the original project objectives are maintained, the project plans change.

If the problem is a major one, it may be impossible to meet all the project objectives: cost, schedule, and end-product performance. Then the project must be replanned to meet the most important project objectives while minimizing adherence to the others. In doing this clear understanding of the criteria, discussed above, is most important.

Another reason for reprogramming stems from customer liaison rather than evaluation. The customer may require some changes in the project after it is planned and executed. Each change should be defined carefully and its impact on project plans analyzed in the general sequence just described.

Changes in project planning and direction should be accomplished as changes or additions to existing plan and direction, not through different means. It is imperative that the communications and administrative

*Reprinted by permission of the Publisher, from *Project Management: How To Make It Work,* Charles C. Martin (pages 24 & 25). Copyright 1976 by AMACOM, a division of American Management Associations.

channels used for initial plans and direction be used for changes. Failure to follow this procedure may result in chaos.

Project management is often looked on as a complicated planning exercise followed by a period in which the project manager and his or her team sit around half-occupied, waiting for results. This is very far from the truth, for coping with the constant changes in the project as it proceeds is often the biggest challenge to project success.

PROJECT REPORTING

The project manager is responsible for reporting on project progress to the customer and to others outside the project who require information about its status. This is consistent with the project manager's responsibility for customer liaison. In a project done under a contract with an outside organization, the project manager is responsible for reporting both to the customer and to general management.

It is important that the internal management and external reporting of the project be based on a common set of data. Maintaining more than one set of books is uneconomical and could lead to misunderstandings among those who should be working together cooperatively. This does not mean that every piece of data available to the project manager should be given to the customer, but it does mean that the data in reports to the customer should be summaries clearly traceable to project data. Further, it does not mean that every early indication of project difficulties should be reported immediately and in detail to the customer, but does mean that no false or misleading impression should be created by the omission of data in reporting.

The project manager's data for report should be based on any special project control systems, on the information systems of the overall organization, and on reports from departments executing project tasks. Departmental reports to the project manager should be based directly on the data the department uses to manage its work. In the case of a matrix organization, any departmental report to higher functional management that reflects on project tasks should be made available to the project manager. Assessments should concern themselves with department tasks and status, and should not be independent judgments on overall project status.

Although reporting is logically the outcome of the evaluation and re-programming activities, it really takes place from the very beginning of the project, and should be approached on a positive basis by all members of the project team. It should be looked on as a constructive opportunity to describe project successes and to get understanding and help for project problems.

EXERCISES

2-1.   Define Project Management.

2-2.   What would you consider as the major benefits for having a periodical review of the status of the project? Comment.

REFERENCES

Buchan, J.R., and Davis, Gordon J. *Project Control Through Network Analysis and Synthesis.* Atlanta: DDR International, 1976.

Cleland, David I., and King, William R. *Systems Analysis and Project Management.* New York: McGraw-Hill, 1975.

Martin, Charles C. *Project Management: How to Make It Work.* New York: AMACOM, 1976.

Chapter
3
PROJECT NETWORK CONCEPT

The heart of critical path methods is a graphical portrayal of the plan for carrying out the project; such a graph shows the precedence relationships, i.e., the dependencies of the project activities leading to the end objectives. This graph is called a network.

The basis for both critical path methods (CPM) and project evaluation and review techniques (PERT) is the project network diagram. The network is essentially an outgrowth of the Gantt or bar chart, which is primarily designed to control the time element of a project as depicted in Figure 3.1. Here the bar chart portrays the major activities comprising the project, their scheduled start and finish times, and their current status. The important ingredients added by the project network concepts are that (1) the dependencies of the activities are noted explicitly, and (2) more detailed definition of activities is made.

It is actually because of the second point that the network concept really became necessary. For modest-sized projects, one can incorporate the dependencies implicitly. However, because of the enormous size of many present-day projects, containing thousands of significant activities, and taking place in widely dispersed locations, the inadequacy of the bar chart is obvious in these cases.

Figure 3.1 illustrates clearly the two major differences in the bar chart and the network diagrams. First, the network shows greater detail. The

15

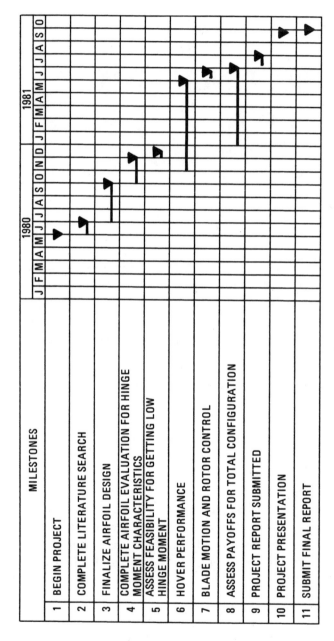

▶ Denotes end of status

(a) Bar chart

FIGURE 3.1   Comparison of Gantt bar chart and project network

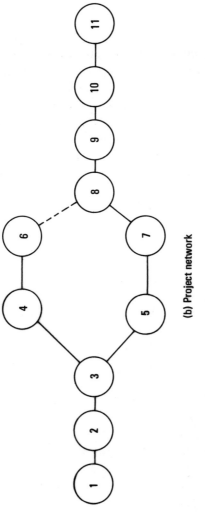

(b) Project network

FIGURE 3.1 Comparison of Gantt bar chart and project network (cont.)

second and more important difference is that the interdependency of the activities is clearly shown. For example, activity 4 can start as soon as activity 3 is finished.

NETWORK DEVELOPMENT

The network concept involves the graphical representation of activities and their precedence requirements. Activities are elements of the project which represent logical subdivisions of the work to be done. The level of detail used depends upon the degree of control desired. For example, if control is desired only on the start of a project, the entire project may be described as a single activity. Precedence requirements indicate which activities must be completed before a given activity can proceed. The network may then be thought of as displaying an orderly, step-by-step series of actions which must be performed successfully to achieve a specific, definable objective.

The basic purpose of the network is to provide a comprehensive picture of the precedence relationships existing among activities. Precedences are determined by comparing the environments created by the completion of an individual activity in the project with the environment necessary for the start of the succeeding individual activities. This step is usually called the "planning phase." Resource availability and customary practice should not be considered as creating precedence relationships. This chapter is limited to those basic rules and procedures of network development required to prepare the first draft of a network. In chapters 4 and 5, the addition of resource availability and customary practice for the development of a final working draft are considered, including the problem of obtaining the most useful level of network detail.

While certain rules and conventions should be followed in preparing networks, it must be realized that accurate and useful networks are based on an intimate knowledge of the project and are the product of good judgment and skill. The rules provide a great deal of flexibility, and the proper use of this flexibility depends on the users—their understanding of critical path concepts and the experience gained through practical applications.

As indicated in chapter 1, there are different systems of networking currently in use. This book emphasized the activity-on-nodes systems.

Two other systems, the activity-on-arrow system and the event system (commonly associated with PERT) are discussed in appendices B and C.

BASIC TERMS AND SYMBOLS

Some of the most common terms and symbols used in the activity-on-node networking system are defined and illustrated below.

(1) An *activity* is a time-consuming element of a project, and it is defined as the work to be done on a project. It is graphically represented by a node, with a short phrase or symbol inside the node indicating the job it represents.

(2) A *node* is any closed geometric figure such as a square, diamond, or circle.

(3) An *arrow* is a line connecting two nodes and having an arrowhead at one end. The arrow designates that the activity at the tail of the arrow precedes the one at the head of the arrow.

(4) A *restriction* is a precedence relationship which establishes the sequence of activities. When one activity must be completed before a sec-

ond activity can begin, the first is considered to be a restriction on the second. The arrow between the two activities indicates that activity A is a restriction on activity B.

(5) A *network* is a graphical representation of a project plan, showing the interrelationships of the various activities. When the results of time estimates and computations have been added to a network, it may be used as a project schedule (see chapters 4 and 5).

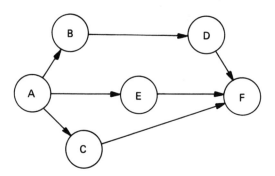

Other useful terms and symbols will be explained at appropriate places throughout this text.

RULES OF NETWORK LOGIC

The few basic rules of networking mentioned in this text may be classified as those common to activity-on-node networking systems.

1. An activity cannot start until all preceding activities have been completed.

2. The compass direction of the arrow has no time meaning, though it is customary to show the arrows going from left to right.

3. The length of the arrow has no correlation to the time duration of of either of the activities it connects.

Interpretation of Rules

Rules 1, 2 and 3 may be interpreted by means of the portion of the network shown below. According to rule 1, this diagram

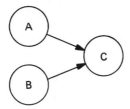

states that "before activity C can begin, activities A and B must be completed." Note that this is not intended to imply that activities A and B must be completed simultaneously.

TIME ESTIMATES

When a network drawing has progressed to the point where the project manager is satisfied that he or she has a workable plan, the next concern is the assignment of activity responsibilities and the making of resource-time estimates. The process of resource-time estimation is directly dependent upon the degree of detail of the activities in the network. As the process of estimation proceeds, it may become necessary to redefine some of the activities to reflect shorter intervals of time that can be accurately, and independently, estimated.

All time estimates are directly related to the resources that are to be used for the activity. All estimates must be based on a normal level of work effort with respect to manpower assigned, shifts worked per day, and days worked per week.

Estimates should generally be made by considering each activity a separate, independent effort, completely isolated from preceding and succeeding activities. It is helpful to have it clearly understood that an estimate is not an inflexible commitment but is simply the individual estimator's experience reflected in a numerical statement and, therefore, may be wrong. The real commitment is to the completion of the project.

Since resources directly influence the time consumed, and the resources available have a direct effect upon the length of time required, it must be assumed that the normal resource level will prevail throughout the span of the activity. This may appear to be a rather broad assumption, but it is a very reasonable one. The estimator must make a judgment as if the activity in question were the only work before him or her. Future/later conflicts may require re-estimates.

Since time estimates are commonly posted directly onto the network, it is easy for the estimator to see the critical path developing. Knowledge of the critical path is almost certain to cause the estimator to consciously or subconsciously modify his or her estimates to obtain some preconceived total duration time.

Then, the object of time estimation is to predict problem areas. If the activities are properly subdivided into short, controllable elements, and one gets out of hand, timely corrective action can be taken before the problem becomes widespread. It is better to be 100% wrong on a 3-week job than to be 15% wrong on a 52-week job. Poor time estimates on small jobs are simply not as dangerous as poor estimates on jobs of long duration where knowledge of the existence of a problem may not be indicated until the project is in serious trouble.

RESOURCE-TIME ESTIMATES

Since resources directly influence the time consumed on a project, and the resources available have a direct effect upon the length of time required, in estimating manpower expenditure, the standard should be a normal working interval such as hours, days, or weeks. One method of estimating activity durations is to estimate the man-hour, or skill-hour, requirements for the activity and divide that figure by the expected work crew size. However, an activity will often include several skills or crafts so that the skill-hours included become difficult to convert to a total activity or

duration time. Generally, the finer the activity breakdown, the more accurate the time estimate can be. It is usually better to have more detail
than is actually required than to risk errors arising from partial dependency relationships and inaccurate estimates.

The resource-time estimating phase is an ideal time to collect the data
that will be needed for analysis and modification during the progress
of the project.

In order to obtain fullest value from critical path planning, scheduling,
and control procedures, it is necessary to express time estimates in terms
of dollars, man-hours, work crew sizes, and equipment. This information
will enable the project manager to make intelligent time-cost trades, reallocate resources, and reschedule activities effectively during the course
of the project.

EXERCISES

3-1.

Activity	Predecessor	Duration
A	None	3
B	None	7
C	None	5
D	A	4
E	C	6
F	A	5
G	B,D,E	3

In establishing the above relationships the following essential questions have been answered:

a. Which other activities must be completed before this activity
can begin?

b. Which activity cannot start until this activity is complete?

c. What other activities can be done at the same time?

Draw the project network.

3-2. Referring to exercise 1, why is networking the cornerstone of CPM
and PERT?

3-3. Careful study and consultation with the people directly involved with various activities has led to the following conclusions: Activities 1, 3, and 5 require no predecessors other than the beginning of the project. Activity 1 must be done prior to either 2 or 10. Activity 4 must follow both 9 and 13, while 14 depends only on 9. Activity 6 can begin only after 2 is completed, and 7 must wait on both 6 and 12. 8 can start as soon as 7 is finished, but 9 depends on both 8 and 11. 11 is ready to begin as soon as 10 and 12 are completed, but 12 has to await completion of both 3 and 5. 13 is preceded by both 8 and 11. Activity 15, the last activity in the project, starts when 4 and 14 are finished. Completion of activity 15 completes the project.

Develop a project network from the information above.

3-4. Given the following relationships, draw the network project:

Activity	Predecessor	Duration (time)
A	None	3
B	None	4
C	None	5
D	None	6
E	B,C,D	5
F	A,B,C,D	7
G	A,B,C,D	8
H	F,G,I	4
I	A,B,C,D	5
J	O,E,N	11
K	B,C,D	7
L	K	6
M	B,C,D	8
N	B,C,D	9
O	A,B,C,D	4

REFERENCES

Awani, Alfred O. *Analysis of a Variable Camber Device for Helicopter Rotor Systems.* Doctoral Dissertation, Lawrence, KA: University of Kansas, 1981.

Buchan, Russell J., and Davis, Gordon J. *Project Control Through Network Analysis and Synthesis.* Atlanta: DDR International, 1976.

Moder, Joseph J., and Phillips, Cecil R. *Project Management with CPM and PERT.* New York: Van Nostrand Reinhold, 1964.

Chapter
4
PROGRAM EVALUATION AND REVIEW TECHNIQUE

PERT was developed initially for scheduling and controlling the Polaris missile project in the late 1950s. Since then it has been used to assist management in planning and controlling many programs and projects that consist of numerous specific jobs or activities, each of which must be completed in order to complete the entire project. A critical task for the project manager in such situations is to schedule and coordinate the activities so that the entire project is completed on time. A complicating factor in carrying out this task is the interdependence of the activities; for example, some activities depend upon the completion of other activities before they can even be started. When we realize that projects can have as many as several hundred specific activities, we see why project managers look for procedures that will help them answer questions such as the following:

1. What is the expected project completion date?

2. What is the scheduled start and completion date for each specific activity?

3. Which activities are "critical," that is, must be completed exactly as scheduled in order to keep the project on schedule?

4. How long can "noncritical" activities be delayed before they cause a delay in the total project?

THE GRAY PORTA-VAC PROJECT

The Gray Company has manufactured industrial vacuum cleaning systems for a number of years. Recently a member of the company's new product research team submitted a report suggesting the company consider manufacturing a cordless vacuum cleaner that could be powered by a rechargeable battery. The vacuum cleaner, referred to as a Porta-Vac, could be used for light industrial cleaning and could contribute to Gray's expansion into the household market. It was hoped the new product could be manufactured at a reasonable cost, and that its portability and no-cord convenience would make it extremely attractive.

Gray's top management would like to initiate a project to study the feasibility of proceeding with the Porta-Vac idea. The end result of the feasibility project will be a report recommending the action to be taken for the new product. In order to complete this project, we will need information from the firm's research and development, product testing, manufacturing, cost estimating, and market research groups. How long do you think this feasibility study project will take? When should we tell the product testing group to schedule their work? Obviously, you do not have enough information to answer these questions at this time. In the following discussion we will learn how PERT can be used to answer these questions and provide the complete schedule and control information for the project.

DEVELOPING THE PERT NETWORK

The first step in the PERT project scheduling process is to determine the specific activities that make up the project. The list of activities for this Porta-Vac feasibility project is shown in Table 4.1. The development of this list is a key step in the project. Since we will be planning the entire project and estimating the project completion date based on our list of activities, poor planning and omissions of activities will be disastrous and lead to completely inaccurate schedules. We will assume that careful planning of the Porta-Vac project has been completed and that Table 4.1 lists all project activities.

TABLE 4.1 Activity List for the Gray Porta-Vac Project

Activity	Description	Immediate Predecessors
A	R & D product design	–
B	Plan market research	–
C	Routing (manufacturing engineering)	A
D	Build prototype model	A
E	Prepare marketing brochure	A
F	Cost estimates (industrial engineering)	C
G	Preliminary product testing	D
H	Market survey	B,E
I	Pricing and forecast report	H
J	Final Report	F,G,I

Note that Table 4.1 contains additional information in the column labeled "Immediate Predecessors." Recall that we mentioned earlier that the project activities have interdependencies. In order to develop the PERT network we will need information about the relationships among the activities. One way to obtain this information is to determine the immediate predecessors for each activity, where the immediate predecessors are all the activities that must immediately precede the given activity. For example, the market survey (activity H) shows activities B and E as immediate predecessors. This simply means that planning the market research (activity B) and preparing the marketing brochure (activity E) immediately precede the market survey.

Figure 4.1 depicts the activities listed in Table 4.1, but also portrays the predecessor relationships among the activities. This figure is the PERT network for the Porta-Vac project. As you can see, a PERT network is simply a graph consisting of circles which are interconnected by several arrows. In general network terminology, the circles are called nodes and the arrows connecting the nodes are called branches. In PERT network the arrows that connect the nodes designate that the activity at the tail of the arrow precedes the one at the head of the arrow, while an activity is represented by a node. The job it represents is indicated by a short phrase or symbol inside the node.

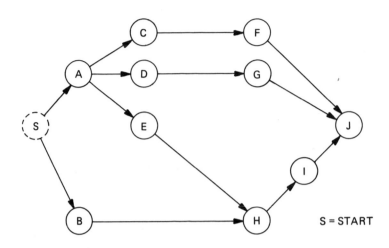

FIGURE 4.1   PERT network of the Porta-Vac project

ACTIVITY TIME

Once we have established a PERT network for our project, we will need information on the time required to complete each activity. This information will be used in the calculation of the duration of the entire project and the scheduling of the specific activities. Accurate activity time estimates are essential for successful project management. Errors in activity time estimates will cause errors in scheduling and project completion date projections.

For repeat projects, such as construction or maintenance projects, managers may have the experience and historical data necessary to provide accurate activity time estimates. However, for new or unique projects, activity time estimation may be significantly more difficult. In fact, in many cases activity times are uncertain and perhaps best described by a range of possible values rather than one specific activity time estimate. In these instances the uncertain activity times are treated as random variables with associated probability distributions, and the PERT procedure is used to provide probability statements about the project meeting specific completion dates.

In order to incorporate uncertain activity times into the PERT network model, we will need to obtain three time estimates for each activity. The three estimates are:

Optimistic time (*a*)—the activity time if everything progresses in an ideal manner

Most probable time (*m*)—the most likely activity time under normal conditions

Pessimistic time (*b*)—the activity time if we encounter significant breakdowns and/or delays

The three estimates enable the manager to make a best guess of the most likely activity time and then express his or her uncertainty by providing estimates ranging from the best (optimistic) possible time to the worst (pessimistic) possible time.

As an illustration of the PERT procedure with uncertain activity times, let us consider the optimistic, most probable, and pessimistic time estimates for the Porta-Vac activities as presented in Table 4.2.

TABLE 4.2 Optimistic, Most Probable, and Pessimistic Activity Time Estimates in Weeks for the Porta-Vac Project

Activity	Optimistic (a)	Most Probable (m)	Pessimistic (b)
A	4	5	12
B	1	1.5	5
C	2	3	4
D	3	4	11
E	2	3	4
F	1.5	2	2.5
G	1.5	3	4.5
H	2.5	3.5	7.5
I	1.5	2	2.5
J	1	2	3

Using the product design activity A as an example, we see that management estimates that this activity will require from 4 weeks (optimistic) to 12 weeks (pessimistic) to complete, with the most likely time being 5 weeks. If the activity could be repeated a large number of times, what would be the average time for the activity? The PERT procedure estimates this average or expected time t from the following formula:

$$t = \frac{a + 4m + b}{6} \tag{4.1}$$

For activity A we have an estimated average or expected completion time of

$$t = \frac{4 + 4(5) + 12}{6} = \frac{36}{6} = 6 \text{ weeks}$$

Equation (4.1) is based on the PERT assumption that the uncertain activity times are best described by a *beta probability distribution*, that is, the equation provides the average time for the special case of a beta probability distribution as the best description of the variability in activity times. This distribution assumption, which was judged to be reasonable by the developers of PERT, provides the time distribution for activity A as shown in Figure 4.2.

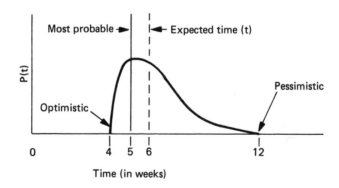

FIGURE 4.2 Activity time distribution for the product design activity A of the Porta-Vac project

For uncertain activity times we can use the common statistical measure of the *variance* to describe the dispersion or variation in the activity time values. In PERT we compute the variance v of the activity times from the following formula:

$$v = \left(\frac{b-a}{6}\right)^2 \qquad (4.2)$$

As we can see, the difference between the pessimistic b and the optimistic a time estimates greatly affects the value of the variance. With large differences in these two values, management has a high degree of uncertainty in the activity time. Accordingly, the variance given by equation (4.2) will be large.

Referring to activity A, we see that the measure of uncertainty, that is, the variance, of this activity is:

$$v = \left(\frac{12-4}{6}\right)^2 = \left(\frac{8}{6}\right)^2 = 1.78$$

The expected times and variances for the Porta-Vac activities, as computed using the data in Table 4.2 and equations (4.1) and (4.2) are given in Table 4.3.

TABLE 4.3 Expected Times and Variances for the Porta-Vac Activities

Activity	Expected Time t (in weeks)	Variance (v)
A	6	1.78
B	2	0.44
C	3	0.11
D	5	1.78
E	3	0.11
F	2	0.03
G	3	0.25
H	4	0.69
I	2	0.03
J	2	0.11
Total	32	

CRITICAL PATH CALCULATIONS

Once we have the PERT networks and the expected activity times, we are ready to proceed with the calculations necessary to determine the expected project completion date and a detailed activity schedule. In our initial calculations we will treat the expected activity time (Table 4.3) as the fixed length or known duration of each activity. Later we will analyze the effect of activity time variability.

While Table 4.3 indicates that the total expected time to complete all the work for the Porta-Vac project is 32 weeks, we can see from the network (Figure 4.1) that several of the activities can be conducted simultaneously (A and B, for example). Being able to work on two or more activities simultaneously will have the effect of making the total project completion time shorter than 32 weeks. However, the desired project completion time information is not directly available from the data in Table 4.3.

In order to arrive at a project duration estimate we will have to analyze the network and determine what is called its critical path. A path is a sequence of connected activities that lead from the starting node to the completion node (J). Since all paths must be traversed in order to complete the project, we need to analyze the amount of time the various paths require. In particular, we will be interested in the path through the network that takes the longest time. Since all other paths are shorter in duration, the longest path determines the expected total time or expected duration of the project. If activities on the longest path are delayed, the entire project will be delayed. Thus the longest path activities are the critical ones of the project, and the longest path is called the critical path of the network. If managers wish to reduce the total project time, they will have to reduce the length of the critical path by shortening the duration of the critical activities. The following discussion presents a step-by-step procedure or algorithm for finding the critical path of a PERT network.

Starting at the network origin (node A) and using a starting time 0 compute an earliest start and earliest finish time for each activity in the network. Write the earliest start time at the beginning of the node and the earliest finish at the end of the node, using activity A as an example, we have:

Let

ES = earliest start time
EF = earliest finish time
t = expected activity completion time

The following expression can be used to find the earliest finish time for a given activity:

$$EF = ES + t \qquad (4.3)$$

Given $ES = 0$ and $t = 6$ for activity A, the earliest finish time was found to be $EF = 0 + 6 = 6$.

Applying this earliest start time rule to a portion of the network involving nodes A, E, H, I, and J, we obtain the following:

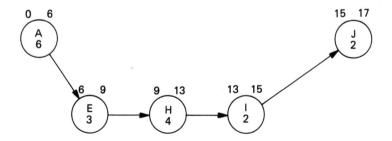

Proceeding in a *forward pass* through the network, we can establish first an earliest start and then an earliest finish time for each activity. The Porta-Vac network with *ES* and *EF* values is shown in Figure 4.3.

Note that the earliest finish time for activity J, the last activity, is 17 weeks. Thus the earliest completion time for the entire project is 17 weeks.

We now continue our algorithm for finding the critical path by making a *backward pass calculation* to find the latest start time for each activity. Starting at the completion point activity J and using a latest finish time of 17 for activity J, we can trace back through the network computing a latest start and latest finish time for each activity.

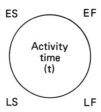

Let

LS = latest starting time
LF = latest finish time

The following expression can be used to find the latest start time for a given activity:

$$LS = LF - t \qquad (4.4)$$

Given an $LF = 17$ and $t = 2$ for activity J, the latest start time for this activity can be computed as $LS = 17 - 2 = 15$.

The following rule is necessary in order to determine the latest finish time for any activity in the network: The latest time an activity can be finished is equal to the earliest (smallest) value for the latest start time of following activities. An example of this is seen in activity A of Figure 4.3.

By comparing the earliest time and the latest start time (or earliest finish and latest finish times) for each activity, we can find the amount

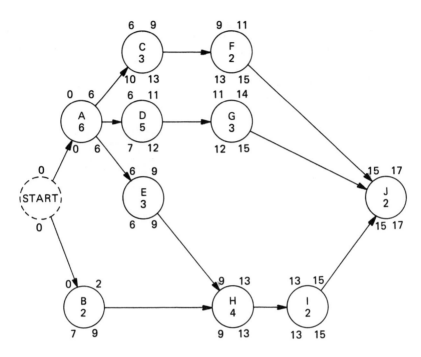

FIGURE 4.3 ES, EF, LS, and LF activity times for Porta-Vac network

of slack or free time associated with each of the activities. *Slack* is de-fined as the length of time an activity can be delayed without affecting the completion date for the project. Using

$$Slack = LS - ES = LF - EF \tag{4.5}$$

we see that the slack associated with activity C is $LS - ES = 10 - 6 = 4$ weeks. This means that the routing activity can be delayed up to 4 weeks (start anywhere between weeks 6 and 10), and the project can still be completed in 17 weeks. This activity is not a critical activity and is not part of the critical path.

Using equation (4.5), we see that the slack associated with activity E is $6 - 6 = 0$. Thus the marketing brochure activity must be held to the 6-week start time schedule. This activity cannot be delayed without affect-ing the entire project. Thus activity E is a critical activity and is on the critical path. In general, the critical path activities are the activities with zero slack. An activity schedule shown in Table 4.4 is helpful in identi-

TABLE 4.4 Activity Schedule in Weeks for the Porta-Vac Project

Activity	Earliest Start	Latest Start	Earliest Finish	Latest Finish	Slack (LS - ES)	Critical Path
A	0	0	6	6	0	Yes
B	0	7	2	9	7	
C	6	10	9	13	4	
D	6	7	11	12	1	
E	6	6	9	9	0	Yes
F	9	13	11	15	4	
G	11	12	14	15	1	
H	9	9	13	13	0	Yes
I	13	13	15	15	0	Yes
J	15	15	17	17	0	Yes

fying the critical path. We see that the critical path for the Porta-Vac project is made up of activities A, E, H, I, and J. In addition, the table shows the slack or delay that can be tolerated for the noncritical activities before they will cause a project delay.

VARIABILITY IN THE PROJECT COMPLETION DATE

During the critical path calculations we treated the activity times as fixed at their expected values; we are now ready to consider the uncertainty in the activity times and determine the effect this uncertainty or variability has on the completion date. Recall that the critical path determines the duration of the entire project. For the Porta-Vac project the critical path of A-E-H-I-J resulted in an expected project completion time of 17 weeks.

Just as the critical path activities govern the expected project completion date, variation in critical path activities can cause significant variation in the completion date. Variation in noncritical path activities will ordinarily have no effect on the project completion date because of the slack time associated with these activities. However, if a noncritical activity were delayed long enough to expend all of its slack time, then that activity would become part of a new critical path and further delays would extend the project completion date. Variability leading to a longer total time for the critical path activities will always extend the project completion date. On the other hand, variability in critical path activities resulting in a shorter critical path will enable an earlier than expected completion date, unless the activity on the other paths becomes critical. The PERT procedure uses the variance in the critical path activities to determine the variance in the project completion date.

If we let T denote the project duration, the T, which is determined by the critical activities A-E-H-I-J, has the expected value of

$$T = t_A + t_E + t_H + t_I + t_J$$
$$= 6 + 3 + 4 + 2 + 2 = 17 \text{ weeks}$$

Similarly, the variance in the project duration is given by the sum of the variance of the critical path activities. Thus the project time variance, V, is given by

$$V = v_A + v_E + v_H + v_I + v_J$$
$$= 1.78 + 0.11 + 0.69 + 0.03 + 0.11 = 2.72$$

This formula is based on the assumption that all the activity times are independent. If two or more activities are dependent, the formula only provides an approximation to the variance of the project completion time. The closer the activities are to being independent, the better the approximation.

Since we know from statistics that the standard deviation is the square root of the variance, we can compute the standard deviation, SD, for the Porta-Vac project. Completion time is as follows:

$$SD = \sqrt{V} = \sqrt{2.72} = 1.65$$

A final assumption of PERT—that the distribution of the project completion time T follows a normal or bell-shaped distribution—allows us to draw the distribution shown in Figure 4.4.

With this distribution we can compute the probability of meeting a specified project completion date. For example, suppose that management has allotted 20 weeks for the Porta-Vac project. While we expect completion in 17 weeks, what is the probability that we will meet the 20-week deadline? Using the normal distribution from Figure 4.4, we are asking for the probability that $T \leqslant 20$. This is shown graphically in Figure 4.5.

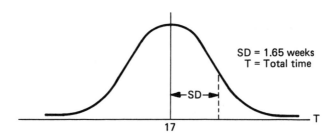

Expected completion time (17 weeks)

FIGURE 4.4 PERT normal distribution of the project completion time variation for the Porta-Vac project

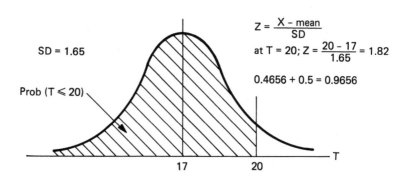

FIGURE 4.5 Probability of a Porta-Vac project completion date prior to the 20-week deadline

By computing the Z value of 1.82 and using the table for the normal distribution (see Appendix A), we see that the probability of meeting the deadline is 0.9656. This is obtained by adding 0.5 to the tabulated number so as to include the left side of the curve (Figure 4.5). Thus, while activity time variability may cause the project to exceed the 17-week expected duration, there is an excellent chance that the project will be completed before the 20-week deadline. Similar probability calculations can be made for other project deadline alternatives.

EXERCISES

4–1. Given the following PERT network:

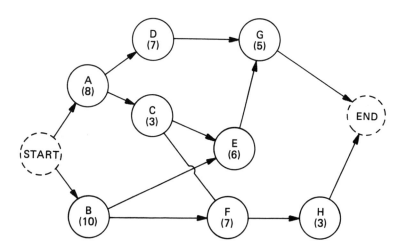

(Activity times in days are in parenthesis)

(a) Identify the critical path.

(b) How long will it take to complete this project?

(c) Can activity E be delayed without delaying the entire project?

(d) Can activity D be delayed without delaying the entire project? If so, how many days?

(e) What is the schedule for activity F (that is, start and completion times)?

4-2. Suppose the following activity times were provided for the PERT network shown in exercise 1:

Activity	Optimistic	Most Probable	Pessimistic
A	6	7	14
B	8	10	12
C	2	3	4
D	6	7	8
E	5	5.5	9
F	5	7	9
G	4	5	6
H	2.5	3	3.5

What is the probability the project will be completed in

(a) 21 days?

(b) 22 days?

(c) 25 days?

4-3. Refer to the Porta-Vac project network shown in Figure 4.1. Suppose Gray's management revises the activity time estimates as follows:

Activity	Optimistic	Most Probable	Pessimistic
A	3	7	11
B	2	2.5	6
C	2	3	4
D	6	7	14
E	2	3	4
F	2.5	3	3.5
G	1.5	2	2.5
H	4.5	5.5	9.5
I	1	2	3
J	1	2	3

(a) What are the expected times and variances for each activity?

(b) What are the critical path activities?

(c) What is the expected project completion date?

(d) What is the new probability that the project will be completed before the 20-week deadline?

(e) Show the new detailed activity schedule (see Table 4.4).

4-4.   A sociologist plans a questionnaire survey consisting of the following activities:

		DURATION IN DAYS		
Activity	Precedence	Mode (m)	Minimum (a)	Maximum (b)
A. Design of questionnaire	—	5	4	6
B. Sampling design	—	12	8	16
C. Testing of questionnaire and refinements	A	5	4	12
D. Recruiting for interviewers	B	3	1	5
E. Training of interviewers	A,D	2	2	2
F. Allocation of areas to interviewers	B	5	4	6
G. Conducting interviews	C,E,F	14	10	18
H. Evaluation of results	G	20	18	34

(a) For this PERT network find the expected activity durations, and
the variances of activity durations.

(b) Draw a network for this project and find the critical path. What
is the expected length of the critical path? What is the variance of
the length of the critical path?

(c) What is the probability that the length of the critical path does
not exceed 60 days?

4-5. A publisher has just signed a contract for the publication of a book. What is the earliest date that the book can be ready for distribution? The following activities with time estimates are involved:

Activity	Precedence	DURATION IN WEEKS Mode (m)	Minimum (a)	Maximum (b)
A. Appraisal of book by reviewer	–	8	4	10
B. Initial pricing of book	–	2	2	2
C. Assessment of marketability	A,B	2	1	3
D. Revisions by author	A	6	4	12
E. Editing of final draft	C,D	4	3	5
F. Typesetting of text	E	3	3	3
G. Preparation of artwork	E	4	3	5
H. Design and printing of jacket	C,D	6	4	9
I. Printing and binding of book	F,G	8	6	16
J. Inspection and final assembly	I,H	1	1	1

(a) For this PERT network find the expected activity durations, and the variances of activity durations.

(b) Draw a network and find the critical path. What is the expected length of the critical path and what is its variance?

(c) What is the probability that the length of the critical path does not exceed 32 weeks? 36 weeks?

REFERENCES

Anderson, David R., Sweeney Dennis J., and Williams, Thomas A. *An Introduction to Management Science*. St. Paul: West Publishing, 1976.

Daellenbach, Hans G., and George John A. *Introduction to Operations Research Techniques*. Newton, MA: Allyn and Bacon, 1978.

Chapter 5
CRITICAL PATH METHOD

$\mathbf{C}$PM is another network-based procedure developed to assist in the scheduling and controlling of multiactivity projects. Like PERT, CPM provides the important capability of allowing the project manager to allocate additional resources to critical activities so that the critical path and thus the project duration can be shortened. However CPM uses only a single estimate of activity times and thus does not consider the effects of uncertainty or variability in the activity times. Because of this, CPM is perhaps most applicable to repeating or recurring projects where experience and historical data provide good estimates of actual activity times. Projects involving construction and maintenance programs have been typical areas for CPM project management applications.

In order to illustrate CPM, let us consider the simple network shown in Figure 5.1. Assume that the network refers to the five activities of a major overhaul and maintenance project for a two-machine manufacturing system. The activities and estimated completion times are presented in Table 5.1.

Critical path calculations for a CPM network are identical to the procedures we used in chapter 4 to find the critical path of a PERT network. Making the forward pass and backward pass calculations, we can obtain the activity schedule shown in Table 5.2. As can be seen, the zero slack times and thus the critical path are associated with activities A-B-E. The length of the critical path and thus the project is 12 days.

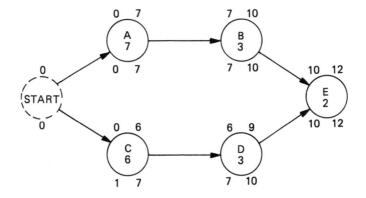

FIGURE 5.1 CPM network of a two-machine maintenance project

TABLE 5.1 Activity List for a Two-Machine
Maintenance Project

Activity	Description	Expected Time (in days)
A	Overhaul Machine I	7
B	Adjust Machine I	3
C	Overhaul Machine II	6
D	Adjust Machine II	3
E	Test system	2

TABLE 5.2 Activity Schedule for the Maintenance Project

Activity	Earliest Start	Latest Start	Earliest Finish	Latest Finish	Slack (LS – ES)	Critical Path
A	0	0	7	7	0	Yes
B	7	7	10	10	0	Yes
C	0	1	6	7	1	
D	6	7	9	10	1	
E	10	10	12	12	0	Yes

CRASHING CAPABILITIES OF CPM

Now suppose that the current production levels make it imperative for the maintenance project to be completed within two weeks or 10 working days. By looking at the length of the critical path of the network (12 days), we realize that it is impossible to meet the project completion date unless we can shorten selected activity times. This shortening of activity times, which usually can be achieved by adding resources such as manpower or overtime, is referred to as crashing the activity times. However, since the added resources associated with crashing activity times usually result in added project costs, we will want to identify the least cost activities to crash and then crash only the amount necessary to meet the desired project completion data.

In order to determine just where and how much to crash activity times, we will need information on how much each activity can be crashed and how much the crashing process costs. Possibly the best way to accomplish this is to ask management for the following information on each activity:

1. Estimated activity cost under the normal or expected activity time.
2. Activity completion time under maximum crashing (that is, shortest possible activity time).
3. Estimated activity cost under maximum crashing.

Let

τ = normal activity time
τ' = crashed activity time (at maximum crashing)

C_n = normal activity cost

C_c = crashed activity cost (at maximum crashing)

We can compute the maximum possible activity time reduction M due to crashing as follows:

$$M = \tau - \tau' \tag{5.1}$$

On a per unit time basis (for example, per day), the crashing cost K for each activity is given by

$$K = \frac{C_c - C_n}{M} \tag{5.2}$$

For example, if activity A has a normal activity time of 7 days at a cost of $500 and a maximum crash activity time of 4 days at a cost of $800, we have $\tau = 7$, $\tau' = 4$, $C_n = 500$, and $C_c = 800$. Thus using equations (5.1) and (5.2), we see that activity A can be crashed a maximum of

$$M_A = 7 - 4 = 3 \text{ days}$$

at a crashing cost of

$$K_A = \frac{800 - 500}{3} = \frac{300}{3} = \$100 \text{ per day}$$

CPM makes the assumption that any portion or fraction of the activity crash time can be achieved for a corresponding portion of the activity crashing cost. For example, if we decided to crash activity A by only 1-½ days, CPM assumes that this can be accomplished with an added cost of 1-½ ($100) = $150, which results in a total activity cost of $500 + $150 = $650. Figure 5.2 shows the graph of the time-cost relationship for activity A.

The complete normal and crash activity data for our example project are given in Table 5.3.

Now the question is, which activities would you crash and how much should these activities be crashed in order to meet the 10-day project completion deadline with a minimum cost? Your first reaction to this

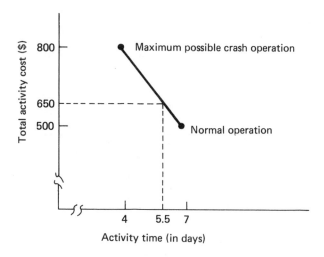

FIGURE 5.2 Time-cost relationship for activity A

question is possibly to consider crashing the critical path activities. While this is correct, be careful because as you reduce the current critical path activity times, another path may become critical.

In a small network you may be able to use a trial-and-error approach to making the crashing decisions, but in large CPM networks you will probably need a mathematical procedure in order to arrive at the optimal decision. A linear programming model is one approach that could be used to analyze CPM network crashing problem (see chapter 6).

TABLE 5.3 Normal and Crash Activity Data for the Maintenance Project

Activity	Normal Time (τ)	Crash Time (τ')	Total Normal Cost (C_n)	Total Crash Cost (C_c)	Maximum Crash Days $(M = -\tau')$	Crash Cost per Day $K = \frac{C_c - C_n}{M}$
A	7	4	$500	$800	3	$100
B	3	2	200	350	1	150
C	6	4	500	900	2	200
D	3	1	200	500	2	150
E	2	1	300	550	1	250
			$1700	$3100		

EXERCISES

5-1. Construct the network for a project having the following activities:

Activity	Immediate Predecessor
A	–
B	–
C	A
D	A
E	C,B
F	C,B
G	D,E

The project is completed when both activities F and G are complete.

5-2. Assume that the project whose network was developed in exercise 1 will be scheduled and controlled by CPM. The activity times are as follows:

Activity	Time (months)
A	4
B	6
C	2
D	6
E	3
F	3
G	5

(a) Find the critical path for the project network.

(b) If the project has a 1-½ year deadline, should we consider crashing some activities? Explain.

5-3. A reactor and storage tank are interconnected by 3" insulated process lines that need periodic replacement. There are valves along the lines and at the terminals, and these need replacing as well. No pipe and valves are in stock. Accurate, as built, drawings exist and are available. The line is overhead and requries scaffolding. Pipe sections can be shop fabricated at the plant. Adequate craft labor is available.

The plant methods and standards section has furnished the following data:

Symbol	Activity Description	Time (hrs)
A	Develop required material list	8
B	Procure pipe	200
C	Erect scaffold	12
D	Remove scaffold	4
E	Deactivate line	8
F	Prefabricate sections	40
G	Place new pipe	32
H	Weld pipe	8
I	Fit up pipe and valves	8
J	Procure valves	225
K	Place valves	8
L	Remove old pipe and valves	35
M	Insulate pipes	24
N	Pressure test	6
O	Clean-up and start-up	4

Careful study and consultation with the people directly involved with the various activities has led to the following conclusions:

Activities A, C, and E require no predecessors other than the beginning of the project. Activity A must be done prior to both B or J. Activity D must follow both I and M, while N depends only on I. Activity F can begin only after B is completed, and G must wait on both F and L. H can start as soon as G is finished, but I depends on both H and K. K is ready to begin as soon as J and L are completed, but L has to await completion of both C and

E. M is preceded by both H and K. Activity O, the last activity in the project, starts when D and N are finished. Completion of activity O completes the project.

(a) Draw a network.

(b) Determine the critical path.

(c) How much time is required?

5-4. Classify the following sequences as logical, conventional, resource-limited or impossible:

(a) check gasoline, check oil

(b) pour tea, add milk

(c) pour tea, add tea

(d) break egg, fry egg

(e) eat egg, fry egg

(f) put on socks, put on shoes

(g) receive goods, pay bill.

5-5. Denise agency is planning an advertising campaign to launch a new product, using posters, television, and newspaper displays. The illustration for the newspaper advertisement will be devised while its accompanying text is being written, and half-tone blocks will be made when both are ready. The blocks will then be sent to the newspapers, but only after the contract for press advertising has been negotiated. This part of the work is then finished.

The poster is to be designed and printed after which, again subject to a satisfactory contract, it will be distributed, so completing this part of the campaign. The script for the television film is to be prepared while the contract with the film company is negotiated. The film, when completed, must be sent to the program company, with whom a separate agreement has to be reached beforehand.

As soon as all these preparations have been made, a press conference is to be arranged for a previously agreed date on which the product will be officially launched. The agency allows a fortnight for drawing up a detailed plan of the campaign, after which its negotiators begin work on the four contracts. Meanwhile, the artists, copywriters, and scriptwriters get on with such work as is possible. Draw a network diagram for the campaign.

5-6. Draw the activity-on-node network for the project described below, eliminating any unneeded relationships:

Activity	Predecessors	Times
A	–	2
B	A	3
C	A	6
D	A	7
E	A,D	3
F	A,B,C	8
G	C,E,F	9
H	D,E	4
I	F,G,H	2
J	I	3

Determine the critical path of the network.

5-7. A company has just developed a new telephone system and wishes to plan its prerelease marketing campaign to be started on May 1. The individual activities are as follows:

Activity		Precedence	Duration (weeks)
A	Project plan, budget prepared and approved	—	1
B	Training of phone service people	A	8
C	Training of salespeople	A	4
D	Sales promotion to distributors	C	4
E	TV and radio advertising brief	A	4
F	TV and radio contract negotiation	E	1
G	TV film making	F	8
H	Radio script taping and approval	F	4
I	Approval of TV film from management	G	3
J	Press and household advertising brief	A	2
K	Press and household advertising contract negotiations	J	1
L	Illustrations, text and block making for press and household advertising	K	4
M	Printing of above	L	4
N	Distribution of phone to distributors	D	2
O	Distribution of phone to retailer	N	4
P	Press Conference	B,O,I,H,M	0

(a) Draw a CPM network, and determine the critical path.

(b) When will the press conference be held at the earliest?

REFERENCES

Anderson, David R., Sweeney, Dennis J., and Williams, Thomas A. *An Introduction to Management Science*. St. Paul: West Publishing, 1976.

Daellenbach, Hans G., and George, John A. *Introduction to Operations Research Techniques*. Newton, MA: Allyn and Bacon, 1978.

Chapter
6
LINEAR PROGRAMMING MODEL OF CRITICAL PATH METHOD

$\mathbf{A}$s we saw in chapter 5, one could use a trial-and-error approach to making the crashing decisions, but in large CPM networks one will probably need a mathematical procedure in order to arrive at the optimal decision. Some network problems can be formulated as linear programs.

Linear programming problems are concerned with the efficient use or allocation of limited resources to meet desired objectives. These problems are characterized by the large number of solutions that satisfy the basic conditions of each problem. The selection of a particular solution as the best solution to the problem depends on some aim or overall objective that is implied in the statement of the problem. A solution that satisfies both the conditions of the problem and the given objective is termed an optimum solution.

While several solution procedures and variations exist for the CPM crashing procedure, the following linear programming model will be used to analyze the Two-Machine Maintenance project for the CPM network utilizing the activity-on-arrow system or the activity-on-node system shown in figures 6.1 and 6.2. First we define the decision variables. Let

X_i = time occurrence of event i, i = 1, 2, 3, 4, 5

Y_j = amount of crash time used for activity j, j = A, B, C, D, or E

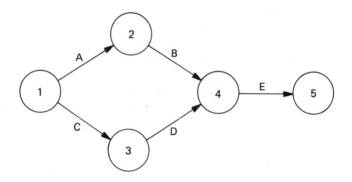

FIGURE 6.1 CPM network of a two-machine maintenance project
(using the activity-on-arrow system)

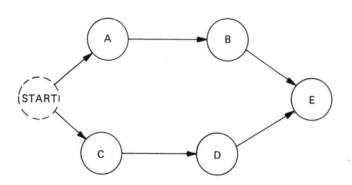

FIGURE 6.2 CPM network of a two-machine maintenance project
(using the activity-on-node system)

Since the total normal time project cost is fixed at $1700 (see Table 5.3), we can minimize the total project cost (normal cost plus crash cost) simply by minimizing the crashing costs. Thus our linear programming objective function becomes:

$$\min \sum_j K_j Y_j \tag{6.1}$$

or

$$\min 100_{Y_A} + 150_{Y_B} + 200_{Y_C} + 150_{Y_D} + 250_{Y_E} \tag{6.2}$$

where K_j is the crash cost for activity j, j = A, B, C, D, E on a per unit time basis.

The constraints on the model involve describing the network, limiting the activity crash times, and meeting the project completion date. Of these, constraints used to describe the network are perhaps the most difficult. The constraints are based on the following conditions:

1. The time of occurrence of event i (X_i) must be greater than or equal to the activity completion time for all activities leading into the node or event.

2. An activity start time is equal to the occurrence time of its preceding node or event.

3. An activity time is equal to its normal time less the length of time it is crashed.

Using an event occurrence time of zero at node 1 ($X_1 = 0$), we can create the following set of network description constraints:

Event 2:

$$X_2 \geqslant \tau_A - Y_A + 0$$

where

X_2 = occurrence time for event 2

$\tau_A - Y_A$ = actual time for activity A

0 = start time for activity A ($X_1 - 0$)

$$X_2 \geqslant 7 - Y_A$$

or

$$X_2 + Y_A \geqslant 7 \tag{6.3}$$

Event 3:

$$X_3 \geqslant \tau_c - Y_c + 0$$

$$X_3 + Y_3 \geqslant 6 \tag{6.4}$$

Since two activities enter node 4, we have the following two constraints:

Event 4:

$$X_4 \geqslant \tau_B - Y_B + X_2$$

$$X_4 \geqslant \tau_D - Y_D + X_3 \tag{6.5}$$

or

$$-X_2 + X_4 + Y_B \geqslant 3$$

$$-X_3 + X_4 + Y_D \geqslant 3 \tag{6.6}$$

Event 5:

$$X_5 \geqslant \tau_E - Y_E + X_4$$

$$-X_4 + X_5 + Y_E \geqslant 2 \tag{6.7}$$

The first constraints, (6.3)–(6.7), are necessary to describe our CPM network (Figure 6.1).

The maximum allowable crash time constraints are:

$$Y_A \leqslant 3 \tag{6.8}$$

$$Y_B \leqslant 1 \tag{6.9}$$

$$Y_C \leqslant 2 \tag{6.10}$$

$$Y_D \leqslant 2 \tag{6.11}$$

$$Y_E \leqslant 1 \tag{6.12}$$

and the project completion date provides another constraint:

$$X_5 \leqslant 10 \tag{6.13}$$

Adding the nonnegativity restrictions and solving the above 9-variable, 11-constraint, (6.3)–(6.13), linear programming model provides the following solution:

$X_2 = 5$ $Y_A = 2$

$X_3 = 6$ $Y_B = 0$

$X_4 = 8$ $Y_C = 0$

$X_5 = 10$ $Y_D = 1$

          $Y_E = 0$

Objective function = $350

This solution requires that we crash activity A 2 days ($200) and activity D 1 day ($150). Thus the total crashed project cost is $1700 + $350 = $2050. The crashed activity schedule for the Maintenance CPM project is given in Table 6.1. Note that all activities are critical.

Resolving the linear programming model with alternate project completion date [constraint (6.13)] will show the project manager the costs associated with crashing the project to meet the alternate deadlines.

Due to the substantial formulation and computational effort associated with scheduling and controlling large projects, most applications of PERT and CPM involve the use of computer programs developed to perform the appropriate network analysis. (For more information on linear programming, refer to a text on operations research or management science.)

TABLE 6.1 Crashed Activity Schedule for the Maintenance Project

Activity	Crashed Time	Earliest Start	Latest Start	Earliest Finish	Latest Finish	Slack
A	5	0	0	5	5	0
B	3	5	5	8	8	0
C	6	0	0	6	6	0
D	2	6	6	8	8	0
E	2	8	8	10	10	0

EXERCISE

6-1. For the CPM project of exercise 2 in chapter 5, suppose that the following crash data is available:

Activity	Normal Time	Crash Time	Total Normal Cost ($ x 10³)	Total Crash Cost ($ x 10³)
A	4	2	50	70
B	6	2	40	55
C	2	1	20	24
D	6	4	100	130
E	3	2	50	60
F	3	3	25	25
G	5	3	60	75

(a) Show a linear programming model that could be used to make the CPM crash decisions if the project had to be completed in T months.

(b) If $T = 12$ months, what activities should be crashed, what is the crashing cost, and what are the critical activities?

REFERENCES

Anderson, David R., Sweeney, Dennis J., and Williams, Thomas A. *An Introduction to Management and Science*. St. Paul: West Publishing, 1976.

Chapter
7
NETWORK COST
PROJECTIONS AND
CONTROL

The results of the planning and scheduling stages of the critical path methods discussed in chapter 5 provide a network plan for the activities making up the project and a set of earliest and latest finish times for each activity. The addition of cost and manpower to the basic time-oriented network system provide cost and manpower data directly related to the work sequence and time schedule. Such an addition is aimed at making it possible for project management to predict overruns or underruns in project costs and manpower expenditures, and to have sufficient supplementary information concerning critical areas to act effectively.

Various experts have questioned whether cost versions of the network-based systems are compatible with traditional cost-accounting methods and whether such network systems should replace existing systems. At present, cost extensions of network systems are not seen as replacing existing accounting systems, but as complementing them by being useful cost-planning, control, and reporting devices for individual projects. This does not imply that reporting systems would be duplicated, but that existing systems would be adapted to provide time, cost, and manpower information in integrated formats. Hence, at best, time/cost/manpower versions of the network-based system would offer management substantial increases in cost and manpower planning and control capability with minimal changes in input methods. The development of the various procedures to be introduced in this chapter is based on the following cost and time definitions:

Activity direct costs includes the costs of the material, equipment, and direct labor required to perform the activity in question. If the activity is being performed in its entirety by a subcontractor, then the activity direct cost is equal to the price of the subcontract.

Project indirect costs may include, in addition to supervision and other customary overhead costs, the interest charges on the cumulative project investment, penalty costs for completing the project after a specified date, and bonuses for early project completion.

Normal activity time-cost point—The normal activity cost is equal to the absolute minimum of direct costs required to perform the activity, and the corresponding activity duration is called the normal time (as used in the basic critical path planning and scheduling). The normal time is actually the shortest time required to perform the activity under the minimum direct cost constraint, i.e., this rules out the use of overtime labor, etc.

Feasible time-cost points is any combination of direct costs and activity performance time which can be scheduled. It is assumed that the choices made are optimal, in that the direct cost is the lowest of all possible direct cost associated with the stipulated activity performance time, and that, correspondingly, the activity performance time is the lowest possible for the stipulated direct costs.

OBJECTIVES OF TIME/COST/MANPOWER APPLICATION

The network-based system which includes cost and manpower dimensions is aimed at relating the activities to be accomplished to the schedule constraints, manpower requirements, and financial information. The network plan, which is a realistic and understandable model of the project, provides the framework within which to correlate these factors. The network system lets the planner link these elements of information together, and compare the actual expenditures of time, labor, and funds with the projected ones. Using the operational time/cost/manpower system, those responsible for the project could prepare the present integrated information to managers for review to facilitate decision-making.

The general objectives of the integrated network-based system are:

1. To provide a sound basis for the development of valid time, cost, and manpower estimates that reflect the actual resources available.

2. To aid in determining whether resources should be applied to best achieve time, cost, and technical performance objectives.

3. To provide a system for early identification of those project areas with the greatest potential schedule slippage and/or cost overruns to facilitate action before trouble develops.

It also enhances management's ability to determine at various levels of the organization:

1. Whether current time and cost estimates for the entire project are within allowable (contract) limits.

2. Whether the project plan is consistent with current schedule and cost commitments, and, if not, the extent of the differences.

3. Whether planned allocations of manpower and other resources of overtime are realistic.

4. Where resources can be reallocated via trade-offs among the activities of the project to expedite accomplishment of pacing activities.

5. What impact slippages (delays) or changes in the ongoing project will have on the availability and allocation of resources.

ENUMERATIVE AND PREDICTIVE PROJECT MODEL

The enumerative and predictive project model is designed to provide a common framework for cost estimation, actual cost accumulation, cost forecasting and comparison of actual and estimated or planned costs for individual or group activities. The basic objectives and capability of the project model may be characterized as:

1. Comparison of expected and actual costs

2. Predictions of future costs

3. Isolation of trouble areas (i.e., projected overruns or underruns)

4. Dynamic correlation of time, cost, and manpower information

Figure 7.1 shows the basic nature and functioning of the model. Time, cost, and manpower requirements are estimated for each activity or work package in the network. As the project progresses, actual expenditures are accumulated and recorded by activity or work package. This procedure enumerates costs already incurred and predicts costs to completion and at completion. In addition, distributing these costs across the activities lets project management isolate the components of this cost data by activity and time period. These data form the basis for corrective actions or replanning, and can be useful as an aid to budgeting. Typical initial data requirements for the extended project (in addition to the previously discussed time data) might be:

1. Direct man-hours and associated costs for each work package.
2. Other direct expense items (e.g., materials, travel) to be applied to the work package.
3. Various codes as needed to further differentiate the data and/or assist in its collection by department, function, labor classifications, etc.
4. Estimated or committed subcontract costs. These categories are only representative: specific input requirements in any given case would be tailored to the specific information needs. As activities are completed, the estimated expenditures (time, cost, and labor) are replaced by actual expenditures when computing remaining expenditures. Thus, with a regular reporting cycle, project management can continually access the validity of plans in terms of time, cost, and manpower. In addition, a quantitative forecast of manning requirements may indicate critical periods in which manpower may be over or under the practical limits of staffing. Project management can then consider whether to hire, lay off, or reassign personnel or to provide for overtime work.

Depending upon the level of detailed inputs furnished, project management can obtain a variety of project outputs for use in planning and control. Included are such output as:

1. Expected manpower requirements by time, period, organization, etc.
2. Evaluation of proposed or actual changes in resources levels

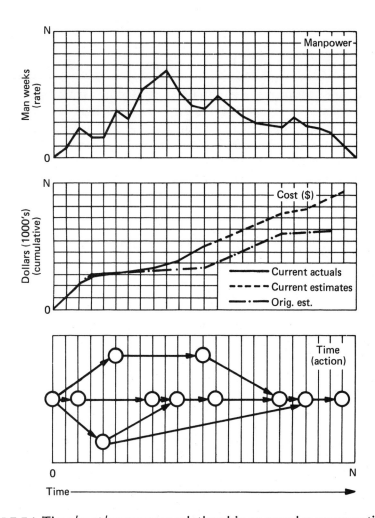

FIGURE 7.1 Time/cost/manpower relationship as seen by enumerative
and predictive project model

3. Expected direct costs in a variety of categories
4. Regular time/schedule outputs, including critical and slack paths, expected completion time, etc. (see chapter 5)

ILLUSTRATIVE EXAMPLE

The network cost projections can be illustrated by assuming the following project data presented in Table 7.1 as an all early start schedule. Now consider that the project manager wants to know the weekly cash requirements expected to be incurred in carrying out the project. If we assume that the project starts on Monday, during the week activities A, B, C, H, one-third of D, and one-fourth of E should be completed as follows:

The total cost for the first week is:

$$(A) + (B) + (C) + (H) + \frac{1}{3}(D) + \frac{1}{4}(E)$$
$$= (425 + 635 + 885) + (600 + 860 + 540) + (920) + (135 + 115)$$
$$+ \frac{1}{3}(460) + \frac{1}{4}(850 + 355)$$
$$= 1945 + 2000 + 920 + 250 + 153 + 301 = \$5,569$$

The weekly expected cash requirements for the early start schedule are:

Week 1	Week 2	Week 3
$5,569	$5,570	$2,531

and the cumulative total is:

Week 1	Week 2	Week 3
$5,569	$11,139	$13,670

At this point the first cost computation is made, which is the summation of all estimated costs by time period. One may also elect to make the summation based on latest start time (LS). These computations will result in curves, similar to that shown in Figure 7.2, which define the range of feasible budgets.

Now a particular budget curve lying somewhere between the earliest start and latest start curves is usually desired. Such a curve may be deter-

TABLE 7.1

Activity		Duration	Earliest Start Time	Earliest Finish Time	Level	Cost ($)
A	Appraisal of book				01	425
	by reviewer	4	0	4	02	635
					03	885
B	Initial pricing of book				01	600
		1	0	1	03	860
					04	540
C	Assessment of	2	1	3	05	920
	marketability					
D	Revisions by author	3	4	7	06	460
E	Editing for final draft	4	4	8	07	850
					08	355
F	Typesetting of text	2	7	9	07	550
					08	1045
G	Preparation of art work				09	690
		1	9	10	10	650
					11	410
H	Design and printing				12	135
	of jacket	2	2	4	13	115
I	Printing and binding				14	645
	of book	3	10	13	15	605
					16	1315
J	Inspection and final				17	445
	assembly	2	10	12	18	345
					09	190

mined by inspecting the project network for activities which, for one reason or another, should start at some time between their earliest start and latest start times (as shown in Figure 7.2). The cost curve then may be recomputed on the basis of the schedule start times.

TIME/COST TRADE-OFF MODEL

The time/cost trade-off model is based on the assumption that there is a relationship between the dollar cost and the expected completion time for each activity. This relationship is expressed as a mathematical model used to evaluate variations in the resource information. During the proposal stage, when they must determine funding levels, the managers get alternate time and cost options for the entire project. They decide on the best schedule, using the time/cost trade-off model. After they have selected the best schedule and established funding levels, they use the resource allocation model to allocate resources in detail among the activities of the project. Finally, as work progresses, the system is used to re-optimize the total time or cost objectives for the project and then to reallocate resources if the project must be accelerated or slowed. The basic inputs to the time/cost trade-off model are alternate feasible time/cost points for each activity; these points denote the various levels of effort that could be applied to an activity and the expected duration for each level of effort.

Typically, planners determine a normal time and cost for each activity. In addition, a crash (minimum) time and related crash cost are established for each activity. The procedure then determines the critical path, and begins to shorten this longest path through the network. The relationship established by the normal crash time and cost estimates allows the project manager to select the most economical activity on the critical path: the activity which provides the most time reduction for the fewest dollars. After a given activity has been crashed, the network is reanalyzed to determine the new critical path; this process continues until the minimum project duration is obtained—when all activities on the final critical path have been crashed (see chapter 5).

The results of this procedure plotted on a time/cost chart produce the direct project cost curve shown in Figure 7.3. The indirect project cost curve is plotted (overhead, interest charges, loss of revenue, etc.), and

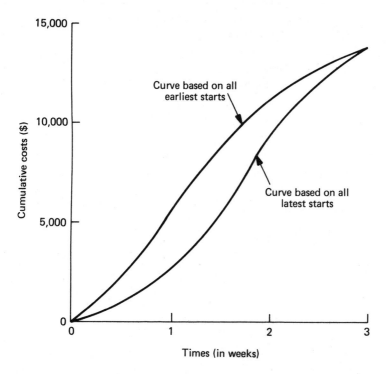

FIGURE 7.2 Sample—cumulative cost curves

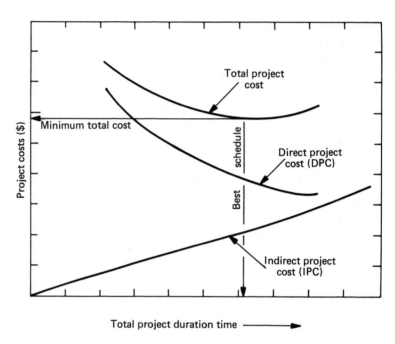

FIGURE 7.3 Determination of Best Project Schedule

these two curves are then summed to produce the total project cost curve. The best project schedule can be selected and established from this final curve. This model is impractical to the extent that it assumes the given network is the best way to plan the project. Actually, revision of the network to reflect improved plans is almost always the way time is saved.

PROJECT OUTPUTS

Too often in the past, the advantages of completion of a project within or before the planned date has largely been offset by overruns which far exceed planned budgets. Such situations occur in environments in which it is impossible to correlate time, cost, and manpower plans in a meaningful way. Conversely, staying within the budget loses significance if there are serious schedule slippages. Hence, the most important objective of the network-based time/cost/manpower system is the correlation of time, cost, and manpower elements to permit trade-offs among these factors to achieve the best total plan. The planner achieves this objective by integrating plans against the work breakdown structure, and presenting the interrelationships among them in the dynamic form of the network plan. The interplay among the planning elements can be shown by the project outputs in coherent statements which management can use.

NETWORK PROJECT COST OUTPUTS

The network project cost outputs are not accounting reports, as usually defined by finance people; rather they are project-oriented cost reports which give managers the visibility to relate resource expenditure to time schedules for project status and control. The network project cost outputs also give a projection of current plans to provide predictions of time/ cost/manpower status when the project is finished.

The cost output possibilities of the integrated system are:

1. By automatically comparing actual work cost with the established budgets in force, the output can show dollar overruns or underruns to date.

2. It can forecast dollar overruns or underruns for selected points to completion, and at completion; this is done by comparing budgets with actual costs plus current estimates for work not started that leads to selected points and to the end objective.

3. It can show the effects of cost plan variances on schedules if cost data are projected at the same time as the relevant current time-only outputs.

The cost outputs can also be used to substantiate estimates, because they can present the data in terms of activities, work packages, or cost categories such as labor dollars or material; other formats management requires, such as costs by organization, by work breakdown hardware element, or by contract, can also be used. The planners can make the data more useful by providing summaries of them with an appropriate amount of detail at various work breakdown structure levels. Using the work breakdown structure as a basis for structuring system outputs, planners can design reports that provide an apparent audit trail; the trail can extend from gross summaries at higher levels down to the pertinent activity of work package account detail which might be the source of a deviation.

PROJECT MANPOWER OUTPUTS

Manpower requirements comprise a major element of a project plan, to be considered both in administrative and technical planning and in cost projection and planning. Therefore, manpower data has a special significance in the resources plan and in the display of project outputs. When the planners acquire direct labor estimates for the plan in cost estimating, they can also secure project outputs. These outputs can highlight areas of particular management interest, such as the actual and planned manpower use computed by skill, organization, time increment, or hardware item; labor costs can be computed in the same terms. This information can be used for management planning, or for periodic analysis of performance against budgeted manpower resources. Various types of manpower information can be produced as system outputs:

1. Labor (expressed in man-hours, days, or weeks) overruns or underruns determined by comparing actual expenditures with budgeted manpower for the work completed.

2. Forecasts of labor overruns or underruns at selected points in the project as well as at completion, computed by comparing allocations with actual expenditures plus current estimates for work not yet started.

3. Effects of variance in the manpower plan on costs and schedule, produced by simultaneously projecting manpower and cost data with the relevant activity/time data.

4. Comparison of the anticipated distribution of manpower requirements or rate of use of overtime (man-loading charts) with the known manpower resources available.

5. Current measures of the number of men being charged to various account details for comparison with plan.

As with the financial information, manpower data can be presented and correlated in a variety of ways with the relevant network time and cost data to give project management the knowledge it needs. A plan can simulate proposed or actual changes in any of the factors (time, manpower, or dollar costs) to assess the impact on project objectives, and to make it easier to consider alternate courses of action.

EXERCISES

7-1. Refer to the illustrative example in chapter 5, and assume that after 10 days the following have occurred:

Activity	Duration	ES	EF	Level	Expected Cost ($)	Actual Cost ($)
				01	380	430
A	7	0	7	02	500	450
				03	635	645
				01	175	175
B	3	7	10	03	200	220
				04	325	300
C	6	0	6	05	500	510
D	3	6	9	06	200	160

What is the new expected total project cost?

REFERENCES

Archibald, Russell D., and Villoria, Richard L. *Network-Based Management Systems (PERT/CPM)*. New York: John Wiley and Sons, 1967.

Moder, Joseph J., and Phillips, Cecil R. *Project Management with CPM and PERT*. New York: Van Nostrand Reinhold, 1964.

Chapter
8
TIME-SCALED NETWORKS AND RESOURCE PROFILES

It has been observed that most people when first learning to use the critical path network have considerable difficulty in fully understanding all the ramifications of the technique. By far the most effective method of presenting the full range of critical path scheduling possibilities is time scaling. Before the development of PERT, the "bar chart" concept of scheduling had been more widely used. Figure 8.1 shows an example of the critical path bar chart. A time scale critical path network has advantages arising from the network logic concept.

A great deal of resource allocation can be done manually with a time-scaled network segment. This frequently permits the project manager to bypass the use of a computer entirely with no loss of information or any time lag. The allocation of resources is really the basis for scheduling. All resources, if allocated intelligently, are utilized subject to some form of constraint. The logical and systematic placement of resources leads to schedules that will maximize project progress with a minimum of wasted effort, time, and cost. Time-scaled networks effectively portray project progress against the selected schedule. Concurrent activities, with conflicting resource needs, are obvious and the real meaning of slack is vividly illustrated.

The real advantage of time scaling is the ease of interpretation it allows. No tool, technique, or procedure has value unless it is implemented effec-

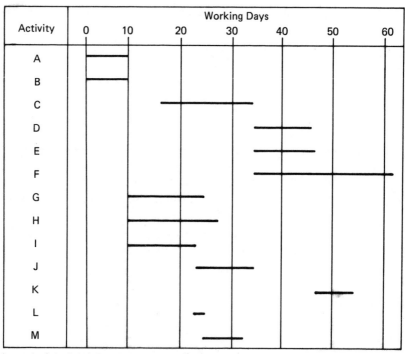

Legend: Scheduled duration ▬▬▬

FIGURE 8.1 Critical Path Bar Chart

ively. The time-scaled network is the quickest, easiest, and most lastingly useful route to full implementation of critical path methods.

Time-scaled networks have the activities represented in proportionate length along the horizontal axis. The length of each activity represents its expected duration. The location of the beginning part of each activity represents its scheduled start time and the placement of the activity end point is the finish time. Each activity can, of course, be located anywhere in the allowable interval for its performance. If an activity does not consume all the time allowed for completion, then it has slack. Slack time is usually shown as a dashed line between the actual and allowable start and/or end points. A time scale illustration is shown in Figure 8.2.

The first step in converting a free body network to a time-scaled network is the selection of a proper scale. It is desirable, though not necessary, to choose a scale so that the shortest activity durations show up clearly and are long enough to permit clear identification. The scale selected should permit two updating periods to be displayed on a work sheet of reasonable length.

Integrally associated with the selection of a time scale is the choice of an updating period. The "best" updating period is a function of many variables, such as possible delay penalties, the effect of external factors on activity durations, and the number of near critical paths in the network. In addition, it may be difficult or costly to bring together all the people required for a thorough progress evaluation except at certain times. Each critical path schedule user usually requires about two projects completed to arrive at the updating period best suited to his or her particular needs. The construction industry, on small projects such as residential housing and small commercial buildings, has found a one-week updating period about right for their needs. Larger projects tend to less frequent intervals for a complete update and use a less formal prog-

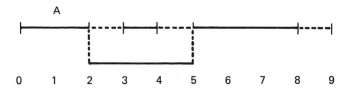

FIGURE 8.2 A Time-Scaled Network

ress check and schedule adjustment in between updates. Complex, tightly scheduled, or highly time-cost related projects may need to be updated at the end of each shift. In general, the more variability inherent in the progress of a project the shorter the updating period.

Consider the activitiy-on-node (A-O-N) network shown in Figure 8.3. The activity-on-node presentation includes all the necessary symbols, computations, and details required for basic network usage. When drawing the time-scaled network, a decision must be made concerning the initial placement of activities. The first draft usually is most easily and quickly done by assigning all activities to begin at the earliest start time or at the latest start time and subsequently adjusting to a final schedule. Assume that the first draft of the time scaling of Figure 8.3 is to be done with all earliest starts. Let one scale unit equal one time unit. Place activity A at time zero and extend for two scale units.

Activity B is on the critical path. It is usually easiest to place the critical path activities first and then fit the remaining activities to the critical path. Now showing activity B added yields

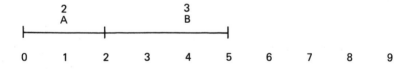

The remaining critical path activities are D and F. Their addition to the network results in

Activity C is on a slack path. This means that if the activity is scheduled at its earliest start time it will be complete before the start of its successor on the critical path, activity D. However, activity E can, and will,

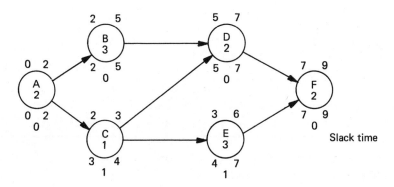

FIGURE 8.3 A-O-N Project Network

start as soon as C is complete, since all activities have been directed to begin as soon as possible. This situation is shown as

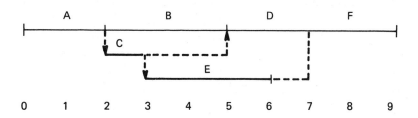

Here the predecessor requirement of E before F is also shown and completes the time-scaled network. The dashed lines represent precedence relationships that contain slack time. The horizontal length component of the dashed line represents time. Vertical displacements have no meaning except to note the precedence constraints and have no time significance.

If the orientation of activities is changed to all latest start time, the network will appear as:

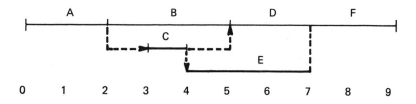

RESOURCE PROFILES

The time-scaled network can readily be used to show the variations in resource levels (manpower, equipment, etc.) used as the project progresses.
In fact, the time scale can be used to determine the best slack activities
to shift in order to attain the best resource utilization. While the time-
scaled network is not a direct scheduling mechanism, it is essential as a
component of the scheduling techniques used later. Figure 8.4 shows the
resource profiles of several different resources in a project. An additional
method of adjusting resource usage is to "split" an activity, that is, an
activity in progress is stopped and the resulting freed resources are used
elsewhere. Another possibility is to reduce or increase resources on a
particular job in order to attain some objective such as smooth utilization of resources or to expedite or delay completion of an activity
(see figures 8.4 and 8.5).

The value of time-scaled networks for presentation to top management
is well documented. Claims that time-scaled networks are too much
trouble or not worth the effort are based on inadequate knowledge or
experience, or in situations where there are no restrictions in the number
of skilled people or special equipment. The procedure outlined here sug-
gests that it is well worth the nominal increment of effort to use time-
scaled critical path networks solely for their value as training aids and
for better understanding and acceptance.

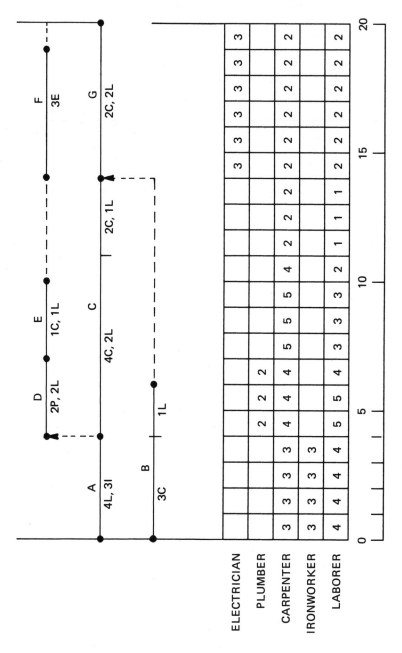

FIGURE 8.4 Original Resource-Time Chart Showing Five Resource Profiles

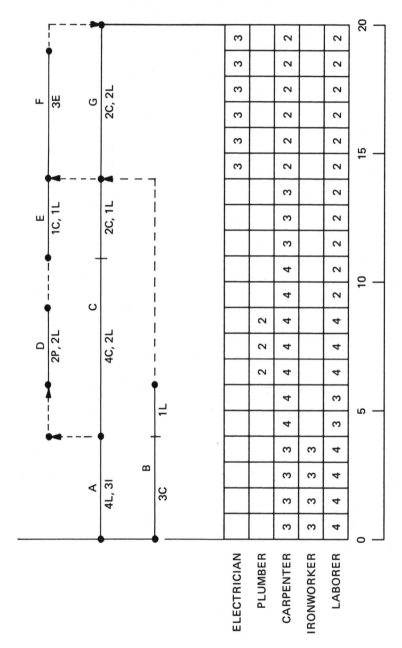

FIGURE 8.5 Revised Resource-Time Chart of Figure 8.4 Showing Improved Resource Utilization

EXERCISES

8-1

Activity	P	Duration	Men Required
A	–	2	3
B	–	4	3
C	–	4	2
D	A	3	2
E	A	8	5
F	A	18	4

Activity	$\overline{P}$	Duration	Men Required
G	B,D	3	3
H	C	4	5
I	C	5	3
J	H	7	6
K	G,I	6	5
L	E	6	7

Make a time-scaled network for the above project, putting all activities on latest start. Show the manpower utilization schedule for this project schedule. Redraw the network, making intuitive shifts to improve the manpower utilization schedule. (Note: $\overline{P}$ = Predecessor)

8-2.   Time scale the following work.

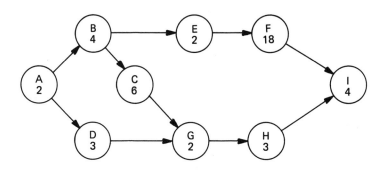

If the following normal resource levels are applicable, modify the time-scaled network representation to incorporate these levels. (Level = Number of workers required.)

Activity	Level	Type
A	3	C
	2	L
B	4	P
C	2	C
	1	L
D	2	L
E	3	C
	1	E
F	1	E
G	2	E
H	1	E
	5	C
I	4	C
	2	L

Would shifting of activities improve the man-power utilization schedule?

8–3.

Activity	Predecessor	Duration
A	–	2
B	A	4
C	B	6
D	A	3
E	B	6
F	E	1
G	C,D	3
H	F,G	2

(a) Draw the activity-on-node network for the project described.

(b) Time scale the network on early start time.

8–4. Referring to exercise 5–6, draw a time-scale network.

REFERENCES

Awani, Alfred O., and Schweikhard, W.G. *Planning, Scheduling and Controlling Techniques in Engineering Project Management* (unpublished). Lawrence, KS: University of Kansas, 1980.

Buchan, Russell J., and Davis, Gordon J. *Project Control Through Network Analysis and Synthesis*. Atlanta: DDR International, 1976.

Chapter
9
PROJECT PROPOSALS

Project proposals preparation utilizing critical path method are based on the various project planning and scheduling techniques discussed in the text, except perhaps that these techniques are applied with less detail than would normally be used on a project that is definitely to be executed. If the project is to be executed, the proposal network serves as a framework for developing a detailed plan and schedule to be used in carrying out the project.

In cases where the project completion time is specified in the contract, critical path methods are useful in determining a project plan which will meet the time specification. It may turn out that this plan requires the use of certain time-saving features which add unexpected costs, or risks, to those which would normally be required to complete the project tasks. For example, if performance time is extremely critical, "crash" time performance of critical path activities may be required. In addition, it may be necessary to perform certain activities concurrently which would normally be performed in series. An example of this is shown in Table 9.1 and Figure 9.1, in which a "normal" plan and an expedited plan are shown for the same project. The added risks of the expedited plan over the normal plan must, of course, be considered in preparing the proposal cost estimate.*

*From Project Management with CPM & PERT by Joseph Moder and Cecil Phillips, Copyright 1964 by Van Nostrand Reinhold Company, reprinted by permission of the publisher.

TABLE 9.1 Hypothetical Rocket Project

Symbol	Activity	Duration (months)	PREDECESSOR Normal Plan	Expedited Plan
A	Analysis	6	–	–
B	Construction of model	4	A	A
C	Final design	4	A	A
D	Drafting	3	B,C	C
E	Design review	2	B,D	B,D
F	Fabrication	6	E	E
G	Environmental test	4	F	F
H	Flight test	5	G	G

If the performance times for the activities which make up the project are subject to a considerable amount of random variation, then the PERT statistical approach is appropriate. As described in chapter 4, the basic project plan can be developed using single time estimates of the activity performance times. Then by obtaining optimistic and pessimistic time estimates for the activities on the critical path, the approximate probability of completing the project on schedule can be computed. If this probability is low, even when an expedited plan such as shown in Figure 9.1 is used, then entering into such a contract would indeed be risky. If it is also known that contract specifications and time requirements are reasonable, then the project does not embody the necessary "technology" to pursue this contract satisfactorily. However, if the probability of meeting the scheduled times is high using the expedited project plan, but the probability is low using the normal plan, then one can interpret the latter as indicating the chances that some or all of the extra expenses involved in the expedited plan will be required to complete the project on schedule. The ideal situation would, of course, be a high probability of meeting the schedules using a "normal" project plan.

A number of organizations use critical path methods routinely, in varying degrees of detail, in preparing project proposals. Also, it is not uncommon for a contracting agency to require the contractor to include a project network and schedule along with other bid documents.

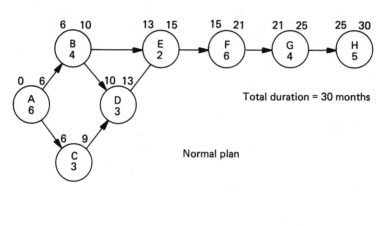

Total duration = 30 months

Normal plan

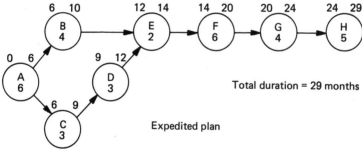

Total duration = 29 months

Expedited plan

FIGURE 9.1 Normal Plan and Expedited Plan for a Hypothetical
            Rocket Project

WRITING THE PROJECT PROPOSAL

The essence of writing any project proposal is the objective or what is intended to be accomplished. An objective is an action to be attained. Objectives tell what will be done. For example, the objective of this book is "to prepare a manual for interested individuals instructing them how to use project management techniques."

Most project proposals require the following elements:

Abstract of the project

Statement of the problem and justification

Review of relevant literature

Objectives to be accomplished

Procedures or methodology to achieve the objective

Project evaluation

Recommended dissemination procedures

Staffing needs

Budget requirements

The above elements will be examined in greater detail.

Abstract of the Project

An abstract can be defined as a "letter of intent" concerning the totality of the idea. Writing and evaluating the project abstract is the first step toward the preparation of the final project proposal. The abstract should only be one or two pages in length and should provide the following information:

The problem of the idea

Objectives of the proposal

A brief set of procedures by which the objectives could be implemented

The type of evaluation that might be utilized

A short discussion of the organization's needed commitment to implement the idea

Estimated costs

In some projects, the evaluation component need not be specified explicitly since it would be implied in the specification of the objectives. Preparation of the abstract should be done with care and completeness since in many cases it often serves as the letter of intent.

Illustrative Example—Abstract Model

1. *Title*: Economic Analysis of the Investment in Project Management Education
2. *Investigator*: Esther Gray
3. *Estimated Cost*: $56,260
4. *Objectives*: This study will examine the problem of the compatability between the benefits from project management education to the individual (private returns) and to society (social returns) in light of the egalitarian principles of American society. The approach consists of analyzing the role of project management in the context of an economy in which the economic value of human time is increasing.
5. *Methods and Procedures*: The study is to develop more fully the economic explanation of the secular increases in the economic value of human time. This largely theoretical endeavor will look at how project management education contributes to increases in the supply of quality attributes in persons and how project management changes as the demand for these attributes change.
6. *Significance of a Career in Project Management Education*: Discussions for the returns to project management education are central to the career educational program's concern for the relationship between project management educational experience and expereince in the world of project work. This research will include a discussion of policy and practice recommendations that will follow from the findings of the theoretical study. Possible areas to be addressed include the influence of project management education on individual decisions outside the project work.

Statement of the Problem

The problem statement must explain why the proposed project should be funded. Remember, you are attempting to convince a panel of judges that your problem is more worthy of support than that of someone else. This is what competitive funding is all about—all applicants are in direct competition with each other. The project manager who takes the effort to review some situation as it has existed and then speculates about future conditions made possible by that project will have that proposal judged higher on the problem section than one who does not adequately develop the significance of the problem.

The statement of the problem should be written in clear, concise terms. It is in this section that a reviewer will be convinced of the worthiness of the project.

Review of Relevant Literature

Any well developed proposal must contain a review of relevant studies, research or curriculum materials. The review should be a closely related orientation to the general problem. Major studies should be cited and briefly summarized. Critical analyses should be noted for those empirical studies selected for review. The review provides one means by which the project manager may establish evidence to provide justification for the study or the methodology being used to accomplish the objectives.

Objectives

As has been stated previously, the essence of a project proposal is a set of well-specified objectives. Each objective should be stated in a simple sentence and should be a statement of what will be accomplished. Objectives are needed to convey the notion of action. It will be the objective which reviewers will examine in detail.

Procedures or Methodology

The needs and objectives of the project are all implemented through the procedures. Procedures or methodology are means by which a project manager carefully articulates how the project will be conducted. Explicit details must be presented to convince the funding organization that the objectives can be accomplished.

There are several different types of methodologies which can accomplish a set of objectives; some general examples are listed below:

Survey

Experimental design

Curriculum development projects

Staff development projects

Case studies

Project Evaluation

All projects must be evaluated to determine if the stated objectives were met. Evaluation should be as simple as possible and should focus on the accomplishment of the project objectives only. The ultimate outcome of the project will be the fruition of the stated project objective.

An internal project evaluation should address how effectively the objectives were accomplished, problems which developed that were unanticipated. In short, internal project evaluation is selecting what will be judged and then judging these items by using predetermined criteria.

While in many smaller projects formative evalation will be adequate, i.e., using evaluation as a "feedback" mechanism, formative designs require a constant monitoring of project activites. The project manager then attempts to make adjustments where needed so that the project may progress at an efficacious rate.

A complementary aspect to the project evaluation procedures is the preparation of a project time-line. The time-line may take many forms, including sample work plans, task-identification plans, flow charts, or PERT charts.

Time-line (see Figure 9.2) or flow charts graphically illustrate activities to all project staff. The chart is really prepared to aid the project manager to coordinate necessary activities, and such a chart becomes a helpful guide for project evaluations.

Regardless of the type of project, the evaluation plans should be specified in the project proposal and should always be aimed at the objectives, since they specify what is to be done.

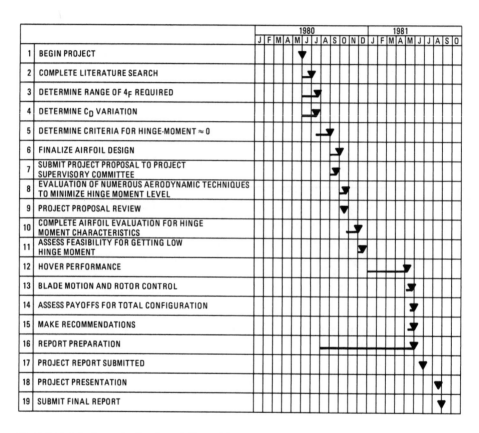

FIGURE 9.2 Sample Project Time-Line

Dissemination Procedures

The proposal should state how the results of the project will be made known to a wider audience. All project managers are required to submit a final report. In most cases, this report will be the actual project description. It should contain the following:

Need for the project

Objective

Procedure

Results

Conclusions and recommendations

Staffing

The project manager is responsible for the total administration of the project, including the writing and submitting of the final report. If the project has other personnel, each position should be described with a listing of major responsibilities of those persons. If consultants are needed they should be identified. A short description of the professional or technical competencies of all personnel should be provided, so that the reviewer will be able to judge the relative professional merits of the project staff. With large projects, a detailed vitae should be included for all principal personnel.

Budgeting Requirements

It is most essential that the project manager makes a reasonable estimate of fiscal needs. Enough detail should be presented to show why the money is requested to conduct the proposed activities.

All personnel who will be paid from the grant or funding as well as those who will contribute in time-sharing should be listed. This should include the project manager, assistants, consultants, etc. The percent of time on the project, the annual salary of the persons, and the amount to be paid each individual for the duration of the project should be stated.

The budget requirements may constitute one or all of the following elements:

Employee benefits (include salary)

Cost sharing

Travel

Supplies and materials

Services

Communication

Equipment

Other direct costs

Indirect cost

SUBMITTING THE PROPOSAL

The proposal must either arrive on the established due date or be post-marked by a specified date or it will be automatically rejected. Secretarial help, duplicating, signature, and final submission must be planned well in advance of the deadline date. This requires coordinating the efforts of several people so that your proposal moves on an established schedule.

If one is a novice at grant writing, it might be helpful to prepare a task-time line chart. All tasks would be identified on such a chart. In this manner all activities could be articulated, culminating with the final proposal being submitted on time.

A great deal of information has been provided in this chapter to aid the project manager or other persons who would like to prepare a project proposal. The project proposal serves as a framework for developing a detail plan and schedule to be used in carrying out a project.

EXERCISES

9-1. Define the following terms:

Abstract
Formative evaluation
Objective
Proposal

9-2. How do the project abstracts differ from the project proposal?

REFERENCES

Awani, Alfred O. Doctor of Engineering Project Proposal for the Analysis of a Variable Camber Rotor. Lawrence, KA: University of Kansas, 1980.

Moder, Joseph J., and Phillips, Cecil R. *Project Management with CPM & PERT*. New York: Van Nostrand Reinhold, 1964.

Orlich, D.C., and Orlich, R.O. *The Art of Writing Successful R. & D. Proposal*. Ridgefield, CT: Redgrave Publishing, 1977.

Chapter
10
PROJECT PERSONNEL SELECTION

SELECTING THE PROJECT MANAGER

One of the most important ingredients of a successful project is the right project manager. Selecting this person is a particularly formidable task because each project has a unique set of circumstances that tends to demand a unique set of qualifications in its manager. In addition, the job has many more dimensions than most managerial posts. Where the project is large and involves many different parts of the organization, the task of finding the right leader approaches complexity in the filling of a general management post. Some of the factors to be considered involve expert knowledge and skill, experience, personal characteristics, and reputation.

Selecting the right project manager should not be a job of paralyzing subtlety: the best project manager is one who is most likely to get the job done well. But the main idea must never be lost.

First of all, relative importance must be assigned to the various "good" characteristics evaluated in the context of the project at hand. Even then, the person with the best personal qualifications may not be the best selection, for reasons to be seen below; selecting too good a person should be avoided; the person should be matched to the job.

Not only should the project manager have the qualifications for the job, but his or her fitness should be readily apparent. If at all possible, the person should be known to potential team members as a proven manager and a dynamic leader. He or she should be known to the other executives of the organization as a prudent executive willing to explore complicated issues on a rational basis to get at the best overall answer. When bringing strangers onto the scene, more careful preparation and more visible manifestations of top management support will be necessary.

Since many projects are carried out under continuing contracts to a customer or are sought under competitve conditions, the preferences of the customer in general and the customer's project manager in particular are most important. A proposal may become a winner because the designated project manager has a long history of honest and successful work with a counterpart on previous projects. Or a government project manager may feel that a particular technical issue is the key to project success; the competitive proposal that designates a project manager who is an expert in the critical field is surely in a preferred position, at least for the area.

One subtle criterion for project manager selection may be derived from examining the value of project success and failure in both the long and short run. In some projects, to achieve success is excellent, and to achieve great success is only a little better; to fail is a disaster. For this environment, the solid citizen and proven performer is the natural selection.

On the other hand, success may not pay if the product does not come in first; in this case, great success will be magnificent, for the winner takes all. Here, the brilliant project manager is the right choice, for if he or she botches the job he or she is no worse off than the competent plodder who comes in second; if the manager wins, the selection is a success.

Looking at the time dimension, one would want a project/program manager who would succeed in the short run and leave behind a constructive atmosphere for future projects and related interpersonal relationships. However, some projects require so much urgent attention for successful schedule performance that the brilliant, heavy-handed driver is the right choice. Alternatively, the clear-thinking manager who can optimize costs and schedules and technical performance may not be the right choice, whereas the big spender will get the job done better or faster under conditions of great urgency.

SELECTING THE PROJECT TEAM

The selection of the project team can best be done in three phases. First, the project manager is selected by general management, usually after consultation with the heads of the divisions that will play a key part in the project. Second, each functional manager to be assigned to the project (for example, the project chief engineer) should be selected by a joint action of the project manager and the head of the corresponding functional division. At the same time, members of the project staff who will report directly to the project manager in jobs having no affiliation with any function may be selected during this phase if they are to be drawn from functional divisions. Third, the rest of the project team can be selected by joint action of the project functional manager, the functional division head, and the project manager.

General management must remain directly responsible until the entire team is selected and approved. A reasonable set of policies for selecting the team should be established. Whatever the policies may be, it is important that they be communicated clearly to the project manager and the functional heads.

Elaborate or formal written policy directives can be dispensed with where verbal direction will suffice; it is essential only that all concerned get the same message—whatever it is. Even if written directives are issued, it is desirable that preliminary discussions include the general manager and all key executives so that everyone will interpret the document properly. In addition, these discussions should emphasize that selecting an adequate project team is everybody's responsiblity, not just the project manager's.

Prior guidelines should also be established. These need not be very formal, but some projects may have higher priorities than others, and various activity within a project may have varying priority rank relative to functional objectives. All these conditions should be acknowledged.

General management should remain available throughout the entire selection process for decision-making in cases of appeal or disagreement. This is the first real opportunity for disagreement between the project manager and functional heads, and if conflict does arise it should be taken care of quickly. A project that starts out in an atmosphere of hostility among key executives is working with a crippling handicap.

Finally, it is good practice that the general manager announce the appointment of the key managers of the project team—and of the project manager, of course, if this has not been done earlier. In so doing, general management declares its support for the whole project; this may encourage wavering functional managers to give enthusiastic support to their counterparts on the project. Furthermore, by placing a seal of approval on the appointees, general management can help mend rifts that may have been opened during the selection process.

DESIRABLE QUALIFICATIONS FOR PROJECT PERSONNEL

Competence is obviously a requirement for any assignment, but it is more important on a project. In many routine jobs, even those demanding fairly advanced professional skills, a person of only modest competence who has diligence, organizational loyalty, and the knack of getting along with people may do a very creditable job. On a project this is simply not the case.

A project is established because special effort is needed to meet its goals. It presents new problems that must be solved in new ways by creative, intellectual effort, not by reliance on the same old techniques. Good decisions must be made rapidly, and this requires clear and fast thinking. That does not mean each project slot must be fitted with the best person of his or her grade in the organization; it does mean that the project position should be staffed with bright, creative people, not with second raters.

People assigned to a project should be able to communicate, to get along with others, and to establish constructive working relationships with new colleagues. In a stable organization, long-term operational practice may have been refined over years to the point where it can accommodate all but the most virulent interpersonal relationships. But on a project, where so much is new, there are no standard solutions. Good decisions must be made on the spot, and this requires good people communicating freely, working together to develop a constructive solution that is both good for the project and generally consistent with good managerial principles. Therefore the shy individual is not usually a suitable choice for a project, even if he or she has the best of motives and real devotion to the project.

Flexibility is another great asset in project personnel. A good slogan to apply during the selection process is "Bureaucrats not needed here." Since a project is full of changes, people who are uncomfortable with change are unlikely to be productive; people who oppose change are likely to be a menace.

At least a moderate sense of organizational sophistication is also required, particularly when a matrix form of organization is employed. People must not be upset by having "two bosses." They must be able to keep the idea clearly in mind that both the project and their functional organization are best served by project success. Apparent disagreements in methods should be resolved so as best to achieve the common goal.

PROJECT PERSONNEL AT THE END OF THE PROJECT

On conclusion of a project, whether in success or failure, all previous commitments made to people on the project must be honored scrupulously, both in letter and in spirit. There are several important reasons for doing so. First, an organization should maintain an ethical stance in all its commitments to its employees, including its project commitments. Second, common sense dictates that available managerial and professional resources be deployed as efficiently as possible; the better people should be in the more responsible jobs and should rank higher in the managerial hierarchy than the less competent.

Finally, future attempts to use project management and to recruit people for projects will be greatly influenced by how people have been treated in past projects. If they have been rewarded for excellent work by being left to fend for themselves at the conclusion of the project, thus making them obviously worse off because of their project assignment, then people will be very reluctant to accept new project assignments. Similarly, functional managers will not volunteer their best people. The whole organization will view these cold personnel reassignments as a negative message about how management really feels about projects.

On the other hand, if people are treated according to the equality principle, then everyone will regard a project tour as a healthy experience in progressive career development. Project assignments will be regarded positively and will be readily filled with good people.

EXERCISES

10-1. What role should the organization play to encourage their employees to accept new project assignments? Discuss.

10-2. Should the functional managers play any role in the project personnel selection? Discuss.

REFERENCES

Martin, Charles C. *Project Management: How to Make It Work.* New York: AMA-COM, 1976.

Moder, Joseph J., and Phillips, Cecil R. *Project Managment with CPM and PERT.* New York: Van Nostrand Reinhold, 1964.

Chapter
11
TYPES OF CONTRACTS

A contract is defined as an agreement that the courts will recognize and enforce. The following list represents the elements of enforceability for most types of contracts in most jurisdictions:

A valid offer

A proper acceptance

Sufficiency of consideration

Parties having legal capacity

Absence of fraud, force, or legally significant mistake

Observance of proper legal form

Consistency with general public policy

Consistency with special rules governing the type of agreement involved

Several basic points regarding the true nature of contracts must now be made. First, almost all contracts are voluntarily carried out by the parties to their mutual satisfaction so that the judicial system never becomes involved. Second, just because one has a legal right to sue for breach of contract does not mean that it is a sound business decision to do so. Before suit is filed, factors such as likelihood of again doing business with the other party, industry attitude about litigious businesses, relative economic strength of the parties, and alternative private means of resolving the dispute should all be considered. Third, in this chapter we will be discussing two basic types of contracts used in the project environment and in the procurement of hardware: fixed-price and cost-reimbursable.

FIXED-PRICE CONTRACTS

The fixed-priced contract reflects an agreement by which the cost is established at its signing and remains fixed provided that no changes in requirements are made and the contractual commitments made by the customer are upheld. Precluding any changes in the contract or specification requirements, the contract price will remain fixed for the life of the contract.

There are four different types of fixed-price contracts which can accomplish a set of objectives, and they consist of the following elements:

Basic fixed-price contract

Fixed-price with escalation contract

Fixed-price with redetermination contract

Fixed-price incentive contract

The above fixed-price type of contracts will be examined in greater detail.

Basic fixed-price contract

The basic fixed-price contract is referred to as a firm fixed-price contract. The firm fixed-price contract is applicable when the purchased item can be identified in detail and when price competition exists. Whereas a firm fixed-price arrangement imposes the greatest risk, it also offers the contractor the incentive and opportunity to realize the greatest profit. In effect, the contractor shares 100 percent in any savings due to cost reduction resulting from his efforts. However, for any major procurement involving engineering or development, where technical unknowns exist, the firm fixed-price contract may no longer be an attractive vehicle for a contractor.

Fixed-price with escalation contract

The fixed-price with escalation contract is applicable when very long delivery schedules are involved. This type of contract is used to protect the contractor against increases in labor rates, materials, overhead, and other costs that are involved in performing under the contract. The escalation feature is usually tied to some official index such as labor rates for the area, basic raw material prices, and other indices.

Fixed-price with redetermination contract

The fixed-price contract with the redetermination feature is applied where large quantities of complex equipment are procured. Its use is justified in cases not only when the engineering and design effort is difficult to estimate but also when the production effort and materials for the large quantitiy of deliverable items are indeterminable. The terms of the contract can be worded to protect the buyer or the seller or both.

There are several variations of the fixed-price contract with redetermination clauses; some general examples are listed below:

Upward and downward adjustment

Downward adjustment only

Redetermination during the life of the contract

Redetermination after completion of the contract

(For more information on the different types of redetermination clauses, refer to Hajek's book listed in the References.)

Fixed-Price Incentive contract

The fixed-price incentive is a form of contract used for major procurements which extend over a long period of time and/or when large production quantities are involved. Its aim is to reward or penalize contractors based on their ability to control cost primarily in manufacturing and general administration.

The fixed-price incentive contract is set up in such a way that a target cost and target profit (largely 10 percent) are established. In addition, a contract ceiling price and price adjustment formula are established during negotiations between the contractor and the customer.

The fixed-price incentive can be expressed by the following illustrative example:

$$\text{Target cost} \ldots\ldots\ldots\ldots\ldots\ldots\$200,000$$
$$\text{Target profit (10\%)}\ldots\ldots\ldots\ldots\quad 20,000$$
$$\text{Ceiling Cost (125\%)}\ldots\ldots\ldots\ldots\quad 250,000$$

The cost-sharing arrangement is 80–20 above and 90–10 below the target cost. If we assume that the contractor experienced an overrun of 20 percent in the contract cost, under the terms of 80–20 for overrun costs cited above, reimbursement would be broken down as follows:

Target cost $200,000

Plus 80% of 40,000 (portion
of overrun assumed by
customer)   32,000

Total reimbursement costs 232,000

Target profit   20,000

Less 20% of 40,000 (portion of
overrun by contractor)   8,000

Total profit..................$ 12,000

Total reimbursement...........$244,000

$$\text{Percent profit} \ldots\ldots\ldots \frac{12,000}{232,000} = \text{about } 5\%$$

If, on the other hand, the contractor completed the contract, incurring a cost of $160,000 ($40,000 less than target cost) under the terms of the cost-sharing arrangement of 90–10 below target cost, the following would evolve:

Target cost $200,000

Less 90% of 40,000 (customer's
portion of saving)   36,000

Total reimbursed costs $164,000

Target profit   20,000

Plus 10% of 40,000 (contractor's
portion of saving)   4,000

Total profit. . . . .$ 24,000

Total reimbursement. $188,000

Percent profit . . . .$\dfrac{24,000}{164,000}$ = about 15%

In no case will the contractor be reimbursed in an amount exceeding the 125 percent ceiling ($20,000 x 125% or $250,000). The $250,000 ceiling figure includes all costs incurred, including profit.

COST-TYPE CONTRACTS

The cost-type contract is used primarily in procurements involving significant R & D effort. This type of contract imposes the greatest risk on the customer, thus it is essential that the contractor selected be established and have a record of proven integrity and reputation. Inherent in the cost-type contract is the intent and execution of the best efforts by the contractor in completing the project.

There are many versions of the cost-type contract but the two most widely used are the cost-plus-fixed fee and cost-plus-incentive fee. These are the cost-type contracts used for procurements from a commercial contractor as contrasted with procurements from a nonprofit organization such as a university.

Cost-plus-fixed fee

The cost-plus-fixed fee contract establishes a fixed fee or profit based on some percentage of an anticipated contract cost negotiated by the customer and contractor and stipulated in the contract. The contractor is usually reimbursed for all allowable costs that are incurred in completing the contract. There are also situations when the contractor is entitled to a fee on costs which exceed the contract cost. The more prevalent situations, when this occurs, are as follows:

1. Change in scope of contract.
2. Costs incurred which are beyond the control of the contractor, e.g., strikes, etc.

Because of the risk that the customer assumes, the cost-plus-fixed fee contract usually incorporates different types of clauses which serve to enable the customer to exert close control over the performance of the contract. Some of the clauses include the following provisions:

1. Customer approves major subcontracts.
2. Allowable costs are defined.
3. Overhead rates are negotiated.

Cost-plus-incentive fee

The cost-plus-incentive fee contract provides for the reimbursement of all allowable costs incurred by the contractor plus a fee based on an incentive formula for performance. It is generally used as a compromise when the offeror is unwilling to enter into a fixed-price contract and when the customer does not want to have a cost-plus-fixed fee contract.

One of the various types of contracts described above will be elected by the customer as the most feasible for a contemplated procurement. The primary objective is to select a type of contract that will promote competition for the procurement.

REFERENCES

Dunfee, Thomas W., Gibson, Frank F., and McCarty, William F. *Modern Business Law.* New York: John Wiley and Sons, 1978.

Hajek, Victor G. *Management of Engineering Projects.* New York: McGraw-Hill, 1977.

Chapter
12
TELEVISION TOWER AND BUILDING PROJECT

The Edgar Company is in the process of preparing a bid for a television station for the erection of a 350-foot high television antenna tower and the construction of a building adjacent to the tower which will be used to house transmission and electrical equipment. Edgar is bidding on the tower and its electrical equipment, the building, the connecting cable between tower and building, and site preparation. Transmission equipment and other equipment to be housed in the building are not to be included in the bid and will be obtained separately by the television station. The site for the tower is at the top of a hill to minimize the required height of the tower, with the building to be constructed at a slightly lower elevation than the base of the tower and near a main road. Between the tower and building is to be a crushed gravel service road and an underground cable. Adjacent to the building a fuel tank is to be installed above ground on a concrete slab. A sketch of the tower and building site is shown in Figure 12.1.

Prior to preparing the detailed cost estimates, Edgar's estimator met with the company's general foreman to go over the plans and blueprints for the job. In addition to preparing a cost estimate, the estimator will also prepare an estimate of the time it will take to complete the job. The television station management is very concerned about getting the station in operation as soon as possible. It has requested that bids be prepared on the basis of the normal time and cost for completing the job,

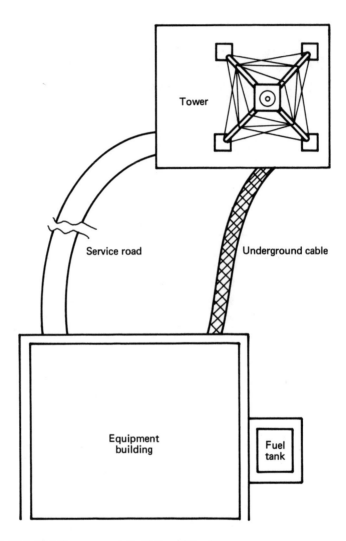

FIGURE 12.1 TV Tower and Building Site Plan

and also for the fastest time (i.e., maximum manpower or resources that could be effectively used on eight-hour work days five days a week) for completing the job and the additional cost that this will entail. The result of the conference between the estimator and general foreman was to determine that the job activities shown in Table 12.1 will be necessary to complete the job. It was agreed that the estimator would prepare time and cost estimates for these activities.

In addition to determining the list of activities, the estimator and foreman discussed in some detail how these activities in Table 12.1 do not necessarily indicate the order in which the work can be performed. In the course of the discussion, the estimator made the following notes:

Survey work and procurement of the structural steel and electrical equipment for the tower can start as soon as the contract is signed.

Grading of tower and building sites can begin when survey is completed.

After tower site is graded, footings and anchors can be poured.

After building site is graded and basement excavated, building footings can be poured.

Septic tank can be installed when grading and excavating of building site is done.

Construction of connecting road can start as soon as survey is completed.

Exterior and interior basement walls can be poured as soon as footings are in.

Basement floor and fuel tank slab should go in after basement walls.

Floor beams can go in after the basement walls and basement floor.

Main floor slab and concrete block walls go in after floor beams.

Roof slab can go on after block walls are up.

Interior can be completed as soon as roof slab is on.

Put in fuel tank anytime after slab is in.

Drain tile and storm drain for building go in after septic tank.

As soon as tower footings and anchors are in and tower steel and equipment are available, tower can be erected.

Connecting cable in tower site, drain tile, and storm drain can be put in as soon as tower is up.

Main cable between building and tower goes in after connecting cable at tower site is in and basement walls are up.

Tower site can be backfilled and graded as soon as storm drain, connecting cable, and main cable are in.

TABLE 12.1 Television Tower and Building Construction Time and Cost Estimate

Activity Code	Activity	NORMAL TIME		FASTEST TIME	
		Weeks	Cost	Weeks	Cost
A	Sign contract and complete subcontractor negotiations	1	–	1	–
B	Survey site	1	$ 1,240	1	$ 1,560
C	Grade building site and excavate for basement	2	1,300	1	1,830
D	Grade tower site	6	6,350	4	8,990
E	Procure structural steel and guys for tower	17	–	17	–
F	Procure electrical equipment for tower and connecting underground cable	24	–	24	–
G	Pour concrete for tower footings & anchors	8	8,310	5	11,670
H	Erect tower & install electrical equipment	7	11,350	5	15,620
I	Install connecting cable in tower site	2	1,740	1	1,950
J	Install drain tile & storm drain in tower site	7	3,600	3	5,100
K	Backfill and grade tower site	2	930	1	1,450
L	Pour building footings	6	3,030	4	4,100
M	Pour basement slab & fuel tank slab	3	1,050	2	1,540
N	Pour outside basement walls	7	2,550	6	2,810
O	Pour walls for basement rooms	2	800	1	960
P	Pour concrete floor beams	2	980	2	1,110

TABLE 12.1 (cont.)

Activity Code	Activity	NORMAL TIME		FASTEST TIME	
		Weeks	Cost	Weeks	Cost
Q	Pour main floor slab & lay concrete block walls	2	1,860	2	2,240
R	Pour roof slab	3	1,740	3	1,960
S	Complete interior framing & utilities	8	9,750	6	11,800
T	Lay roofing	1	270	1	340
U	Paint building interior, install fixtures, and clean up	4	920	3	1,350
V	Install main cable between tower site and building	7	4,360	5	4,540
W	Install fuel tank	1	180	1	220
X	Install building septic tank	2	630	2	750
Y	Install drain tile & storm drain in building site	3	530	2	830
Z	Backfill around building, grade, and surface with crushed rock	2	680	1	850
AA	Lay base for connecting road between tower and building	3	2,560	3	2,970
BB	Complete grading and surface connecting road	2	1,600	1	2,340
CC	Clean up tower site	1	240	1	500
DD	Clean up building site	1	210	1	400
EE	Obtain job acceptance	1	–	1	–
	TOTAL		$68,760		$89,780

NOTE: Costs are direct labor and rental of equipment only.

Backfill around building and grade after main cable is in and after storm drain is in.

Following the meeting with the general foreman, the estimator prepared cost estimates and time estimates for completing the various portions of the job. Estimates for both the normal time in which the work could be completed and the fastest possible time along with the corresponding costs are shown in Table 12.1. The cost figures are for the direct labor and equipment use costs only. Estimated costs of direct materials used in construction and purchased equipment to be installed in the tower are shown in Table 12.2. Company experience had shown that for this kind of job, the following conditions will apply:

Indirect labor cost = 65 percent of direct labor and equipment use cost (Table 12.1)

Overhead Cost = $1000/week

General and Administrative Cost = $1500/week

The company also customarily allowed 15 percent of the total estimated cost for contingencies. Using this information, the estimator prepared analyses for the job: *One for the cost of doing the work at normal rate, and one for the cost of doing the job in the shortest possible period of time.*

TABLE 12.2 Estimated Cost of Materials and Equipment

Item	Cost
1. Structural steel and guys for tower	$41,000
2. Tower electrical equipment and connecting cable	12,800
3. Sand, gravel, crushed rock, and cement	8,400
4. Lumber and millwork	6,800
5. Drain tile and sewer pipe	4,400
6. Septic tank, plumbing fixtures, fuel tank and other hardware	5,100
7. Other miscellaneous materials	5,900
TOTAL	$84,400

The following activity predecessors for the term project were established from the previous discussions:

Activity Code	Predecessor	Activity Code	Predecessor
A	–	R	Q
B	A	S	R
C	B	T	R
D	B	U	S
E	A	V	I, N, O
F	A	W	M
G	D	X	C
H	E, F, G	Y	X
I	H	Z	V, Y
J	H	AA	B
K	J, V	BB	AA
L	C	CC	K
M	N, O	DD	T, W, Z
N	L	EE	BB, CC, DD, U
O	L		
P	M		
Q	P		

TABLE 12.3

Activity Code	Normal Crew Size	Normal Level	Type Normal	Fastest Crew Size	Fastest Level	Type Fastest
A						
B	3	1 2	S R	5	2 3	Surveyor Rodmen
C	2	2	O	3	3	Operator (O)
D	4	4	O	6	6	Operator
E						
F						
G	4	1 2 1	C L I	7	3 3 1	Carpenter Labor Ironworker
H	5	1 1 2 1	E I L C.O	8	2 2 3 1	Electrician I L Crane operator
I	6	2 4	E L	7	3 4	E L
J	2	1 1	O L	4	1 3	O L
K	2	1 1	L O	5	3 2	L O
L	2	1 1	L O	3	2 1	L C
M	2	1 1	C L	3	1 2	C L
N	2	1 1	C L	3	1 2	C L
O	2	1 1	C L	3	3	Carpenter Labor
P	2	1 1	C L	3	1 2	C L
Q	4	1 2 1	C L B	6	1 3 2	C L Bricklayer

TABLE 12.3 (cont.)

Activity Code	Normal Crew Size	Normal Level	Type Normal	Fastest Crew Size	Fastest Level	Type Fastest
R	4	2	C	6	3	C
		2	L		3	L
S	6	1	C	8	2	C
		1	E		1	E
		1	P		1	Plumber (P)
		3	L		4	L
T	2	2	L	4	4	L
U	6	2	PA	8	3	Painter (PA)
		1	E		1	E
		1	P		1	P
		2	L		3	L
V	4	1	O	6	1	O
		1	E		2	E
		2	L		3	L
W	3	1	C.O	5	1	C.O
		1	I		2	I
		1	L		2	L
X	3	1	C.O	5	1	C.O
		1	L		2	L
		1	P		2	P
Y	2	1	O	4	1	O
		1	L		3	L
Z	3	2	O	4	2	O
		1	L		2	L
AA	3	2	O	4	2	O
		1	L		2	L
BB	4	2	O	5	2	O
		2	L		3	L
CC	1	1	L	2	2	L
DD	2	2	L	3	3	L
EE						

PRELIMINARY PLANNING AND SCHEDULING

1. Working at a normal rate, in how many weeks can the job be completed? What should be the bid on this basis if Edgar attempts to obtain a profit of 10 percent before federal income taxes?

Develop the following information:

(a) Construct network using normal time.

(b) Construct a resource-time chart showing the resource profiles.

(c) Calculate forward pass.

(d) Calculate backward pass.

(e) Total slack time.

(f) Time and cost estimate.

(g) Optimize the cost and minimize schedule.

2. What is the shortest (fastest) possible time in which the job can be completed? What should be the minimum bid on this basis if Edgar attempts to obtain a profit of 10 percent before federal income taxes?

3. If the job is obtained and the work is to be completed working at a normal rate, what portions of the work should be supervised most carefully to ensure that the job is completed on time?

4. If the television station management felt that estimated time for completing the job in the shortest or fastest (i.e., maximum manpower/resources that could be used effectively on an 8-hour work day 5-day week) possible time was still too long, what would you recommend?

REFERENCES

Awani, Alfred O., and Schweikhard, W.G. *Planning, Scheduling and Controlling Techniques in Engineering Project Management* (unpublished). Lawrence, KS: University of Kansas, May 1980.

Buchan, Russell J., and Davis, Gordon J. *Project Control Through Network Analysis and Synthesis.* Atlanta: DDR International, 1976.

Chapter
13
PROJECT MANAGEMENT SIMULATION

A project management simulation has been devised to allow the student to participate in a dynamic interactive way; the student plans the project prior to its beginning and then directs the project as it unfolds in response to a series of unpredictable and randomly introduced perturbations and variables that cause the project situations to change as time progresses. The simulation is done in an accelerated time frame where five weeks of simulated time is done in one week of real time. While this simulation does not include the human drama of day-to-day interactions of a real project, it does supply a reasonable representation of week-to-week adjustments that must be made in managing a project in order to keep it on schedule and within the target costs.

The procedures described here allow the student the opportunity to assume the role of a project manager in making decisions throughout the duration of the project. To start with, the project manager will define his or her goals in light of specified bonuses and penalties. The manager will then design an initial schedule to meet these goals, and will select an updating plan which balances the specified degree of project control. Then the manager will simulate progress during the first interval between updates. At the updating point, he or she will reschedule as necessary to meet the goals and to adjust the control process as deemed necessary. The progress simulation-update cycle will be repeated until the project is completed. The costs of the project will be tabulated as a measure of effectiveness of the project manager's decision-making.

During the interval between updatings, the project will be subject to two random delay factors, *weather and absences*, over which the project manager has no control. At the updating point, the project manager has two means of offsetting these delays—the use of overtime and the enlargement of a crew size.

Table 13.1 contains information concerning the plan for the Television Station (term project). Listed are the two factors (weather & absenteeism) which influence the various activities in the project. Table 13.2 lists the factors affecting the project, the probability that a given factor will occur on any given day, the random numbers corresponding to the stated probability of occurrence, and indicates the effect of each factor should it occur. Table 13.3 is the variable project costs weekly summary for recording overtime, manpower augmentation, overhead costs for updating that week and cumulative week.

Table 13.4 is a combined weekly critical activity summary and five weeks' statement. It is made out by the project manager and lists the activities overdue for start or within five weeks of their latest start time. It therefore takes the items from the fourth column (weeks before start date) and adds to them any activities now overdue for starting. Needless to say, if the project is entirely on time, this document becomes a "nil" return; if, however, any critical activity is late (or a near-critical one is becoming late), this table will provide information to that effect and a directive for taking action. The activity node code numbers, activity description, or man/machine week lost, and the reason for being behind schedule are all shown in Table 13.4. This table provides the necessary information of every trouble spot in the project, how serious the trouble is (by giving the critical weeks lost), and the reason for being late. Thus this table then becomes the remedial directive. The project manager or the student has the responsibility of seeing that action is taken to recover the lost time. This action will, of course, depend on the circumstances of the case. It may be necessary to increase the resources being used, to implement overtime or to make some light change in the methods of working; he or she therefore completes the ninth column of Table 13.4.

The project, as stated, is considerably simpler than it is in reality. However, most of the actual control, cost decision, and updating problems that occur in a real project appear here. Consequently, carrying this project to conclusion through simulation will provide a realistic experience in operating a critical path-based project control system.

ROLE OF RANDOM NUMBERS IN SIMULATION

In this section we will show how random numbers can be used to simulate the probabilistic inputs of a model. Specifically, random numbers are used to provide the simulation for the television station tower problem.

Almost everyone who has been exposed to simple random sampling and basic statistics is familiar with tables of random digits or random numbers. Actually, there are complete handbooks that contain nothing but table after table of random numbers. We have included one such table of random numbers in Appendix D. Twenty random numbers from the first line of this table are as follows:

13 68 96 21 91 51 20 66 12 08

The specific digit appearing in a given position is simply a random selection of the digits 0, 1, 2, . . . 9, with each having an equal chance of selection.

If we select random numbers from the table in sets of two digits as they appeared, this will provide us with 100 two-digit random numbers from 00 to 99 with each two-digit random number having a 1/100 (0.01) chance of being selected. While we could select the two-digit random numbers from any part of the random number table, suppose we start by using the last row of random numbers from Appendix D. Our two-digit random numbers would be:

25 57 63 95 94 18 84 06 12

If an event has a known relative frequency of occurrence, such as plumbers being absent from work 1 day out of 10 working days (or 10 days out of each 100 or 20 weeks), then it is a simple matter to assign the same relative frequency of occurrence to numbers in a random number table. Then sampling from the random number table will result in a relative frequency of occurrence of the assigned numbers in a way that corresponds to the actual occurrence of the event in question. This assumes of course that the event in question also occurs randomly and not systematically.

For example, assume that the actual relative frequency of absences of plumbers is 0.10. If two-digit numbers are chosen from the table, the possible value will range 00 to 99, 100 values in all, with all values in the range equally probable. Then let each of the ten values 00 through 09 represent an absence. If a sample from Appendix D resulted in the number 87, it would indicate that the plumber is not absent. A value of 07 would indicate one absence in each 10 working days. The numbers selected previously would indicate only one absence because of the number 05 being in the set. Note that any range of ten digits could represent this same probability of absences (e.g., 10–19, 50–59, 73–82, etc.)

ILLUSTRATIVE EXAMPLE

Since a project network, together with the time and resource data is a model of the actual project, it is easy to simulate actual project progress. *Assume* that a contractor has a network prepared that represents the project of constructing a building. He realizes that while almost all activities are stable and of predictable duration, there are uncertainties involved. One factor which can cause significant delays is the weather. The contractor identifies each activity that could be delayed by inclement weather and found the probability of inclement weather on any day. He checks his records for absenteeism among the various skills and records the relative frequency of occurrence for each skill classification.

In order to proceed with the simulation it is necessary to assign ranges of random numbers to the various factors which can contribute to delays. The simulation of actual occurrences is then determined by the appearance of appropriate numbers in a random number table or as generated by the computer. The random number table in Appendix D is used for this example.

The results of the contractor's finding is summarized below:

Personnel

Type	No.	Prob. Absent	Random Numbers Ranges
Mason	2	0.15	00–14
Carpenter	2	0.20	00–19
Plumber	2	0.20	00–19

Weather		
Probability		*Random Numbers Ranges*
inclement	0.28	00–27

Assuming that we are only looking at the first week of the project of constructing a building, the schedule shows that three activities should occur (activities 1, 2, and 3):

Activity No.	Description	Duration	Crew Size	Skill
1	Lay basement wall	2	2	Masons
2	Frame	2	2	Carpenters
3	Plumbing in ground	3	2	Plumbers

The schedule is:

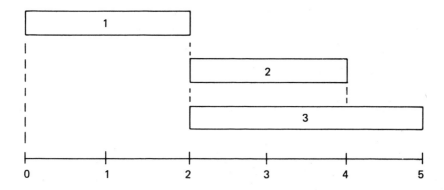

Note that activities 2 and 3 cannot start until activity 1 is complete. Assume that all possible levels of resources provide the same efficiency so that a man-day present is a man-day of progress:

Activity 1 has 2 x 2 = 4 mason-days' work

Activity 2 has 2 x 2 = 4 carpenter-days' work

Activity 3 has 2 x 3 = 6 plumber-days' work

The simulation procedure is: If the situation above were part of the simulation, the steps to be followed would be:

Step 1: Check the weather for the first day. (Pick a two-digit random number from the random number table reading from Appendix D.)

Result: The number picked is 37 which indicates good weather.

Step 2: If the weather is inclement, no work is done on that task. If the weather is good, check to see if the masons report for work. (Pick two-digit random numbers.) First mason: 76-percent for work. Second mason: 24-percent for work.

Step 3: Record the net progress for the first day. Activity 1 progressed as scheduled in a table similar to Table 13.4.

Step 4: Repeating steps 1, 2 and 3 for the second day.
Weather: 51-good weather
Mason: 05-first mason absent
           82-second mason present
One mason-day of progress is recorded.

Step 5: Continue until the project is complete.

PROJECT MANAGEMENT AND CONTROL SIMULATION

Instructions and Ground Rules

The project management and control simulation will be conducted using random number tables to establish the delay factors in the same way as for the foregoing illustrative example. The tasks (activities) to which these factors are to be applied are shown in Table 13.1. The simulation will begin at the 25th week. The roof slab or roof forms (activity R) have just collapsed and the estimated cost in dollars and schedule is $1,740 and five weeks.

Just as in an actual project, certain management policies must be adhered to. Also for the sake of simulation, certain ground rules have been established as follows:

Overtime Policy:

(a) Time and a half for all overtime.

(b) Up to *two hours* of overtime can be performed any weekday from Monday through Friday or ten hours per week and *ten hours* on Saturday.

1. The contract specifies completion time in calendar weeks.

2. Probability of work preventing inclement weather on any given week during this period of time is, according to the Weather Bureau, 0.28.

3. If the project is completed in 45 or less calendar weeks, the contractor will receive a bonus of $500 plus $200 per week for every week less than 45 weeks.

4. If the project takes 46 or more calendar weeks, the contractor must pay a penalty of $500 plus $200 per week for every week in excess of 45 weeks.

5. The work week is from Monday through Friday. Saturday work may be performed only if the project experiences a delay in the preceding weeks due to unforeseen circumstances (e.g., bad weather, absenteeism, etc.) Five weeks of project time will be done in one week of class time. Accelerating ahead of this rate is done at your own risk.

6. On Saturday, crafts (skills) not already on the job that week cannot be used on overtime.

7. A project review and update is to be scheduled at the end of work each class week or as specified by the instructor.

8. Decisions can only be made regarding overtime, added manpower, or changes in your goals at the end of a week and prior to beginning the next week.

9. In case of overtime, record the overtime, manpower augmentation, updating and overhead cost both for that week and cumulatively on Table 13.3.

10. After determining the actual work force on hand for the week, record the progress, the cost incurred, and the remaining work content of the activities on Tables 13.3 and 13.4, respectively.

11. Make new scheduling decisions considering past project progress and continue the progress procedure.

12. Assume that all possible levels of resources provide the same efficiency so that a man-week present is a man-week of progress (as shown in the illustrative example).

13. During the interval between updatings, the project will be subject to two random delay factors which you cannot control—weather, personnel absences and/or special situations introduced by the instructor.

14. The effect of these random variables is to be simulated and the actual progress of the project is to be recorded on a weekly basis. For the general procedure, use the simulation procedure as shown in the illustrative example.

15. Calculate the total cost actually incurred (costs + penalties – bonuses) in carrying out your project.

REFERENCES

Awani, Alfred O., and Schweikhard, W.G. *Planning, Scheduling and Controlling Techniques in Engineering Project Management* (unpublished). Lawrence, KS: University of Kansas, 1980.

Buchan, Russell J., and Davis, Gordon J. *Project Control Through Network Analysis and Synthesis.* Atlanta, GA: DDR International, 1976.

TABLE 13.1 Activity Precedence Listing and Influencing Factors

DESCRIPTION					AFFECTING FACTORS						
					ABSENCE OF						
Activity Code	Normal Working Weeks	Special Instruction	Predecessor	Weather	Iron Worker	Carpenter	Electrician	Plumber	Painter	Operator	
A	1		—								
B	1		A								
C	2		B								
D	6		B								
E	17		A								
F	24		A								
G	8		D								
H	7		E,F,G	X	X		X			X	
I	2		H	X			X				
J	7		H	X						X	
K	2		J,V								
L	6		C								
M	3		N,O								
N	7		L								
O	2		L								
P	2		M								
Q	2		P								
R	3		Q	X		X					
S	8		R			X	X	X			
T	1		R								
U	4		S				X	X	X		
V	7		I,N,O	X			X			X	
W	1		M								
X	2		C								
Y	3		X								
Z	2		V,Y	X						X	
AA	3		B								
BB	2		AA								
CC	1		K	X							
DD	1		T,W,Z	X							
EE	1		U,BB								

TABLE 13.2 Factors, Probabilities of Occurrence, and Costs

1	2	3	4	5	6
Factors *Personnel*	*Maximum Workers Available*	*Probability Absent*	*Corresponding Random Numbers Range*	*Cost of Each Extra Man-Day*	*Fixed One-Time Cost to Obtain Extra Worker*
Labor	—	—	—	—	—
Carpenter	4	0.15	00–14	$30	$35
Electrician	3	0.10	00–09	$40	$30
Plumber	2	0.20	00–19	$36	$25
Painter	3	0.08	00–07	$30	$50
Operator	4	0.10	00–09	$32	$40
Bricklayer	2	0.27	00–26	$28	$30
Ironworker	3	0.10	00–09	$35	$42

Weather	Probability	Random No. Range
Inclement	0.28	00–27
Fair and Mild	0.72	28–99

NOTE: There are two alternatives presently available for expediting an activity.

1. Hire extra workers. This has extra labor cost and a one-time hiring cost per person listed in column 6.
2. Work overtime. This has a premium cost 1½ times column 5.

Maximum Workers Available: That is what we've been told to limit it to. We assume that the office has surveyed the manpower market and finds that there is a high demand for certain skills and no more than the maximum stated will be available from local sources during that time period.

TABLE 13.3 Variable Project Costs

Week	Overtime		Extra Men		Updating		Overhead	
	Weekly	Cumul	Weekly	Cumul	Weekly	Cumul	Weekly	Cumul
1								
2								
3								
4								
5								
6								
7								
8								
9								
10								
11								
12								
13								
14								
15								
16								
17								
18								
19								
20								
21								
22								
23								
24								
25								
26								
27								
28								
29								
30								
31								
32								
33								
34								
35								
36								
37								
38								
39								
40								
41								
42								
43								
44								
45								
46								
47								
48								
49								
50								

Grand
Total

TABLE 13.4 Weekly Critical Activity Summary—Five Weeks' Statement

CONTRACT_____ CONTRACT NO_____ PROJECT WEEK NUMBER_____ DATE_____

1	2	3	4	5	6	7	8	9
Week	Activity Code	Activity Description	Weeks before Start Date	Critical Weeks Lost	Skill Code	Critical Man-Machine Week Lost	Reason for Being Behind Schedule	Action Taken by Project Manager to Recover Lost Critical Weeks

Chapter
14
CASE STUDIES (PROJECTS)

THE OIL REFINERY PROJECT

Part 1

A maintenance schedule is being drawn up for the partial overhaul of a unit in an oil refinery, and the following list of job activities has been compiled:

Activity Code	Activity Description	Predecessor	Duration (hours)
	No. 1 COOLER:		
A	Remove tube bundle from shell	U	16
B	Inspect and gauge shell	A	16
C	Clean tube bundle	A	8
D	Replace tube bundle	B,C	6
P	Test cooler	D	36
	No. 2 COOLER:		
E	Pressure test	U	16
Q	Replace piping after test	E	12

Activity Code	Activity Description	Predecessor	Duration (hours)
	BOTTOM INLETS:		
F	Remove and repair	U	40
R	Re-install	F	8
	HEAT EXCHANGER:		
H	Remove tube bundle from shell	G	16
K	Inspect and gauge shell	H	16
L	Fit replacement tubes to bundle	H	24
M	Replace tube bundle	K,L	8
S	Test and replace piping	M,N	16
	MISCELLANEOUS:		
U	General preparation before any work begins	–	24
G	Regenerate catalyst	U	24
N	Test auxiliary piping	G	4
T	Clean up site after all work has been completed	P,Q,R,S	8

Work on the two coolers, the bottom inlets, the auxiliary piping and the heat exchanger can go on concurrently, but the last two items only must wait until the catalyst has been regenerated.

The test must be carefully scheduled. No. 1 cooler must not be tested until No. 2 has been found satisfactory, although there is no need to wait for the piping to be replaced on No. 2. The heat exchanger test cannot be done until the auxiliary piping has been tested. The shell of a unit cannot be inspected until the tube bundle has been taken out, and no unit can be tested until it has been reassembled.

(a) Draw a network

(b) Identify the Critical Path

(c) How long will it take to complete this project?

Part II

After studying the analysis of the oil-refinery network, the refinery project manager decides to start regenerating the catalyst (activity G) right at the beginning of the project, instead of waiting for the preparatory work (activity U) to be finished.

(d) Will this shorten the overall duration of the project? If so, by how much?

(e) Given that no further modification can be made to the network itself, which individual jobs should now be examined first?

(f) Which event in the original oil-refinery network (above) has the greatest slack time?

Part III

The oil refinery project has been in progress for 48 hours and No. 1 Cooler is causing difficulty. It took 4 hours longer than expected to remove the tube bundle from the shell, and one look at the mess inside convinced the project engineer that the whole cooler would have to be scrapped. It should be possible to get a new unit for replacement within 48 hours and fit it in another 12 and this will be referred to the project manager when he arrives at 9 A.M. Meanwhile the project engineer starts his men on to dismantling the old cooler. The inspector, having no work to do on No. 1 cooler, has looked at the outside of the shell of the heat exchanger. He suspects that it will need a welding job not previously foreseen: about 8 hours work. All other jobs are on schedule.

(g) As the refinery project manager, what action would you take? In particular, would you warn the head office of any delay in getting the plant "on stream"?

DEVOE DETERGENTS PROJECT

DeVoe Detergents Incorporated distributes its main product in 40-gallon (180-litre) drums transported by motor trucks: practically all of the customers take only one drum at a time. Loading full drums on to trucks at the factory dispatch bays is quite simple, but to do it elsewhere is diffi-cult. Normally this does not matter, since only empty drums are collected from the customer. However, a consignment of 600 drums has been found to have a serious fault; the whole consignment has already been delivered and the company is faced with the problem of reloading the drums at each customer's premise, where there are no mechanical aids.

The present method of reloading drums uses the apparatus shown in Figure 14.1, and a mate has to accompany the driver whenever a full drum is to be reloaded (but not otherwise). The driver stops his vehicle with the rear end nearest to the reloading point; he and his mate dismount and go to the rear of the truck. Working together, they remove the ramps in turn from their racks and lay them on the ground, after which they lower the tailboard. Each then takes a ramp and lifts it into its socket: the truck is then ready to receive the drum.

The driver does not like to leave the truck unattended while it is in this state, so he stays with it while his mate goes off to fetch the drum

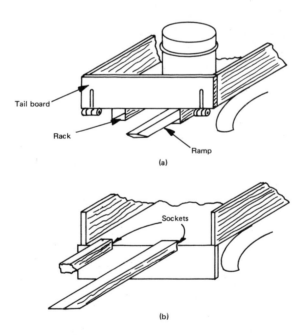

FIGURE 14.1 Reloading drums: (a) truck with tailboard up and ramps
stowed away; (b) tailboard down and ramps in position for
reloading drums

up to the ramps. Then on arrival at the ramp, they both begin to roll the drum up the ramps on to the platform of the truck: this is very heavy work, even for the two men working together, so they rest afterwards. They then climb on to the platform, turn the drum on end, and move it to the required position. They remove the ramps from the sockets, taking one each, then join forces to raise and secure the tailboard and replace the ramps in their racks. Then they return to the cab, thus concluding the cycle of work. A table of the job activities is below:

Activity Code	Activity Description	Duration (seconds)	Predecessor
A	Driver moves from cab to rear of truck	10	W
B	Mate moves from cab to rear of truck	10	W
C	R.H. ramp from rack to ground	18	A
D	L.H. ramp from rack to ground	18	B
E	Lower tailboard	6	C,D
F	R.H. ramp into socket	12	E
G	L.H. ramp into socket	12	E
H	Driver watches truck	120	F
K	Mate fetches drum to truck	120	G
L	Roll drum up ramps	36	H,K
M	Rest	10	L
N	Move drum to position on truck	26	M
P	R.H. ramp to ground	12	N
Q	L.H. ramp to ground	12	N
R	Raise and secure tailboard	6	P,Q
S	R.H. ramp to rack	20	R
T	L.H. ramp to rack	20	R
U	Driver return to cab	10	S
V	Mate return to cab	10	T
W	Lead Time	0	–
Z	End Time	0	A,B

(a) Assuming that the predecessors given in the table above are correct, draw a network diagram of the operations showing the sequential relationships.

(b) Find the minimum duration of the project.

(c) What is the latest starting time for job L?

(d) If job E were to take 18 seconds, all other durations remaining unchanged, by how much, if at all, would the project be delayed?

ANSWERS TO SELECTED EXERCISES

CHAPTER 4

4-2.

Activity	Optimistic	Most Probable	Pessimistic	Variance
A	6	7	14	1.78
B	8	10	12	–
C	2	3	4	0.11
D	6	7	8	–
E	5	5.5	9	0.44
F	5	7	9	–
G	4	5	6	0.11
H	2.5	3	3.5	–

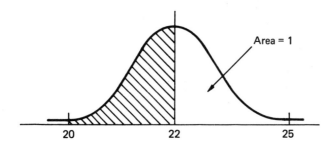

(a) Probability the project will be completed in 21 days:

$$Z = \frac{21 - 22}{1.56} = -.64$$

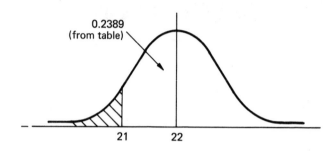

Prob. (Comp. Time ⩽ 21) = 0.5 − .2389 = .2611
(b) Probability of completing in 22 days:

$$Z = \frac{22 - 22}{1.56}$$

Probability = .5 − (Area)
= .5 − 0
Probability = 0.5

(c) Probability of completing in 25 days:

$$Z = \frac{25 - 22}{1.56} = 1.96$$

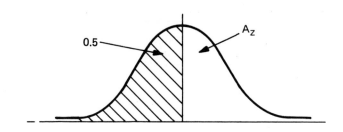

Prob. = 0.5 + 0.4726 (from table) = 0.9726
Probability = 0.9726

CHAPTER 5

5-2.

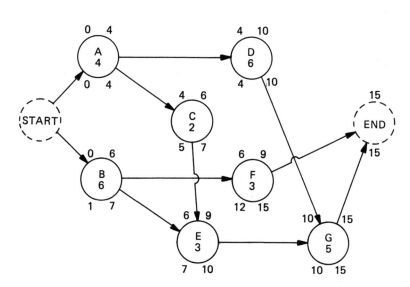

(a) Critical path for the project network: *A - D - G*

(b) No, we should not consider crashing some activities, since the critical path indicated that the project can be completed in 1¼ years, which is less than the 1½ years anticipated.

5-4.

(a) Resource-limited, because usually only one man is available; conventional, in that he could just as easily check the oil first.

(b) Conventional

(c) Conventional, in a different school of thought

(d) Logical

(e) Impossible if "egg" means "one particular egg." Resource-limited, if "egg" means "any egg" and only one is available.

(f) Logical

(g) A sequence required by law is best regarded as logical, but one can pay for goods in advance, and to this extent the sequence is conventional.

CHAPTER 8

8-3.

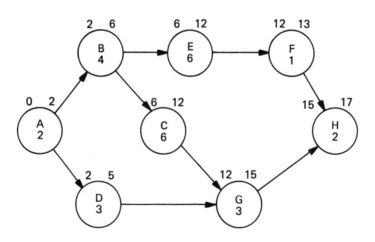

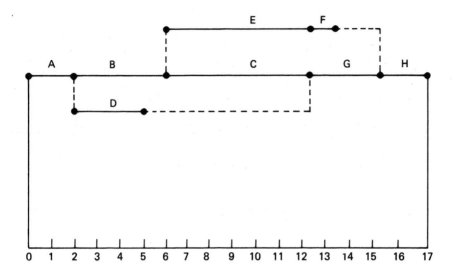

APPENDICES
A
NORMAL
DISTRIBUTION

$\mathbf{T}$he normal distribution is the most important distribution. It is completely determined by two parameters: the expected value of mean, μ, and the variance, σ^2, of the random variable. The normal random variable X with mean μ and variance σ^2 can be expressed in terms of the standardized normal random variable Z with mean 0 and variance 1 for which extensive tables exist (see page 00). The following transformation is used:

$$X = \mu + Z\sigma \tag{A-1}$$

or

$$Z = \frac{X - \mu}{\sigma} \tag{A-2}$$

and

$$P(X \leqslant a) = P(Z \leqslant \frac{a - \mu}{\sigma}) \tag{A-3}$$

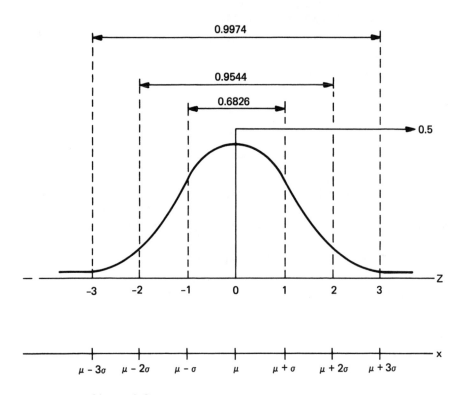

FIGURE A.1. Normal Curve

For continuous distributions the area under the curve equals the probability. As the sum of the probabilities for all possible outcomes is one, the total area under the normal curve is one. We can find the area under portions of the distribution from Figure A.1 as follows:

Boundaries	Area under normal curve between boundaries
$\mu \pm 1.0\sigma$	0.683
$\mu \pm 2.0\sigma$	0.954
$\mu \pm 3.0\sigma$	0.997

To illustrate the significance of the mean and standard deviation, consider the following example.

ILLUSTRATIVE EXAMPLE*

Suppose the useful life of a particular type of airplane was normally distributed with a mean life of 15 years and standard deviation of 2.4 years. How could one obtain random samples from the distribution?

A convenient method is based on the standardized normal distribution. Figure A.2 shows both the standardized normal distribution and the particular useful life normal distribution desired. The deviation of any value of X from the mean of the distribution may be expressed by equation (A.1) or (A.2). From this we see that any point X on a specific distribution (with μ and σ) has an equivalent point Z on the standardized normal distribution. This relationship allows us to relate the standardized normal distribution to any other normal distribution.

In our useful life, two standard deviations above the mean would be at $X = 15 + 2(2.4) = 19.8$ years on the useful life distribution, Figure A.2b. The equivalent point on the standardized normal distribution is:

$$Z = \frac{X - \mu}{\sigma} = \frac{19.8 - 15}{2.4} = +2.0$$

*The Illustrative Example is from *Engineering Economic Analysis* by Donald G. Newman and reproduced with permission of Engineering Press, Inc., the copyright owner.

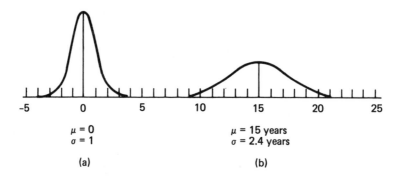

-5   0   5   10   15   20   25

$\mu = 0$ $\mu = 15$ years
$\sigma = 1$ $\sigma = 2.4$ years

(a)   (b)

FIGURE A.2. (a) Standard Normal Distribution and (b) Specific Useful
Life Normal Distribution

This interrelationship means that if we randomly sample from the standardized normal distribution, we can relate this to an equivalent random sample for any normal distribution.

The point on the standardized normal distribution ($\mu = 0$, $\sigma = 1$) is fully defined by specifying the number of standard deviations the point is to the left (negative) or to the right (positive) of the mean. Thus the value of +1.02 would indicate the point is 1.02 standard deviations to the right of the mean.

AREAS FOR THE STANDARD NORMAL DISTRIBUTION

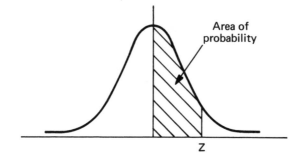

Area of
probability

Z

Entries in the table give the area under the curve between the mean and z standard deviations above the mean. For example, for $z=1.25$ the area under the curve between the mean and z is 0.3944.

z	0.00	0.01	0.02	0.03	0.04	0.05	0.06	0.07	0.08	0.09
0.0	0.0000	0.0040	0.0080	0.0120	0.0160	0.0199	0.0239	0.0279	0.0319	0.0359
0.1	0.0398	0.0438	0.0478	0.0517	0.0557	0.0596	0.0636	0.0675	0.0714	0.0753
0.2	0.0793	0.0832	0.0871	0.0910	0.0948	0.0987	0.1026	0.1064	0.1103	0.1141
0.3	0.1179	0.1217	0.1255	0.1293	0.1331	0.1368	0.1406	0.1443	0.1480	0.1517
0.4	0.1554	0.1591	0.1628	0.1664	0.1700	0.1736	0.1772	0.1808	0.1844	0.1879
0.5	0.1915	0.1950	0.1985	0.2019	0.2054	0.2088	0.2123	0.2157	0.2190	0.2224
0.6	0.2257	0.2291	0.2324	0.2357	0.2389	0.2422	0.2454	0.2486	0.2518	0.2549
0.7	0.2580	0.2612	0.2642	0.2673	0.2704	0.2734	0.2764	0.2794	0.2823	0.2852
0.8	0.2881	0.2910	0.2939	0.2967	0.2995	0.3023	0.3051	0.3078	0.3106	0.3133
0.9	0.3159	0.3186	0.3212	0.3238	0.3264	0.3289	0.3315	0.3340	0.3365	0.3389
1.0	0.3413	0.3438	0.3461	0.3485	0.3508	0.3531	0.3554	0.3577	0.3599	0.3621
1.1	0.3643	0.3665	0.3686	0.3708	0.3729	0.3749	0.3770	0.3790	0.3810	0.3830
1.2	0.3849	0.3869	0.3888	0.3907	0.3925	0.3944	0.3962	0.3980	0.3997	0.4015
1.3	0.4032	0.4049	0.4066	0.4082	0.4099	0.4115	0.4131	0.4147	0.4162	0.4177
1.4	0.4192	0.4207	0.4222	0.4236	0.4251	0.4265	0.4279	0.4292	0.4306	0.4319
1.5	0.4332	0.4345	0.4357	0.4370	0.4382	0.4394	0.4406	0.4418	0.4429	0.4441
1.6	0.4452	0.4463	0.4474	0.4484	0.4495	0.4505	0.4515	0.4525	0.4535	0.4545
1.7	0.4554	0.4564	0.4573	0.4582	0.4591	0.4599	0.4608	0.4616	0.4625	0.4633
1.8	0.4641	0.4649	0.4656	0.4664	0.4671	0.4678	0.4686	0.4693	0.4699	0.4706
1.9	0.4713	0.4719	0.4726	0.4732	0.4738	0.4744	0.4750	0.4756	0.4761	0.4767
2.0	0.4772	0.4778	0.4783	0.4788	0.4793	0.4798	0.4803	0.4808	0.4812	0.4817
2.1	0.4821	0.4826	0.4830	0.4834	0.4838	0.4842	0.4846	0.4850	0.4854	0.4857
2.2	0.4861	0.4864	0.4868	0.4871	0.4875	0.4878	0.4881	0.4884	0.4887	0.4890
2.3	0.4893	0.4896	0.4898	0.4901	0.4904	0.4906	0.4909	0.4911	0.4913	0.4916
2.4	0.4918	0.4920	0.4922	0.4925	0.4927	0.4929	0.4931	0.4932	0.4934	0.4936
2.5	0.4938	0.4940	0.4941	0.4943	0.4945	0.4946	0.4948	0.4949	0.4951	0.4952
2.6	0.4953	0.4955	0.4956	0.4957	0.4959	0.4960	0.4961	0.4962	0.4963	0.4964
2.7	0.4965	0.4966	0.4967	0.4968	0.4969	0.4970	0.4971	0.4972	0.4973	0.4974
2.8	0.4974	0.4975	0.4976	0.4977	0.4977	0.4978	0.4979	0.4979	0.4980	0.4981
2.9	0.4981	0.4982	0.4982	0.4983	0.4884	0.4984	0.4985	0.4985	0.4986	0.4986
3.0	0.4986	0.4987	0.4987	0.4988	0.4988	0.4989	0.4989	0.4989	0.4990	0.4990

Reprinted by permission from *An Introduction to Management Science* by Anderson, David R., Sweeney, Dennis J., and Williams, Thomas A. Copyright 1976 by West Publishing, St. Paul.

B
ACTIVITY ON ARROW
SYSTEM OF NETWORKING

An activity-on-arrow (AOA) network consists of two basic geometric symbols. An arrow, which represents an activity, and a circle or square, which represents an event. The arrow and event symbols each have several distinct properties.

For arrows:

1. The length of the arrow has no correlation to the activity time duration.

2. The compass direction of the arrow has no time meaning, though it is customary to show the arrows going from left to right.

3. No activities (arrows) may be left dangling. Every activity must have a starting event and an ending event.

For events:

1. All events, except the terminal event, must have a following activity.

2. All events, except the first or initial event, must have a preceding activity.

3. An event is a point in time which signals the completion or beginning of one or more activities. It consumes no time or resources.

In addition, the use of *computers* and certain manual operations requires that:

1. Any two events may be connected by no more than one activity.
2. Event numbers must not be duplicated in a network.
3. Networks may have only one initial event (no predecessor) and only one terminal event (no successor). There are certain exceptions to this rule.

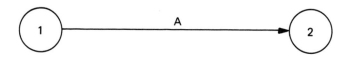

A two-activity network could appear as in either figure below.

Act.	Pred.
A	None
B	A

Sequential A-O-A two-activity network

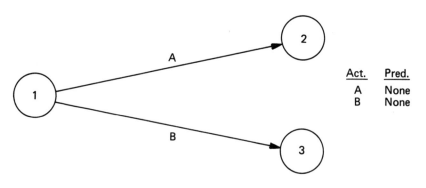

Act.	Pred.
A	None
B	None

Concurrent A-O-A two-activity network

In order to have only one starting and one ending point in the network of the figure immediately above, dummy activities must be used:

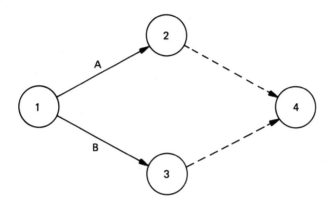

Dummy activities used to attain a single complete event

But it is possible to get by with one less dummy than this:

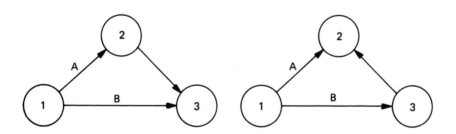

Conservation of dummies

It is necessary to be able to identify each activity by a pair of event numbers, its starting event number, i, and its ending event number, j. Therefore no two activities may have the same pair of event numbers. In the previous networks, activity A would be activity 1-2 and activity B would be activity 1-3.

Dummy activities are required in the A-O-A system to correctly display certain sets of precedence requirements. This is illustrated in the following example. Assume that training of an equipment operator can begin as soon as he is hired and the equipment is installed.

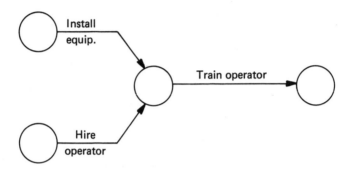

Dependency relationship

Training is to start immediately after installation and is not to be delayed for inspection of the equipment. The equipment can be inspected after installation is complete.

Addition of an activity in sequence

If the "inspect equipment" activity is added to the above "dependency relationship" network, the following relation may result:

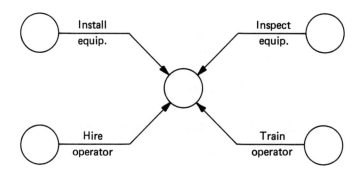

Addition of an activity to a network

But this shows the hiring of the operator unnecessarily holding up the inspection activity. To keep dependency relationships clear, a dummy constant is added.

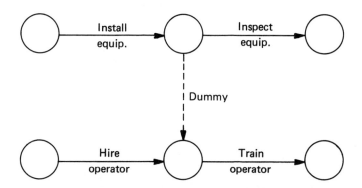

Addition of a dummy to correct a dependency relationship

Now the inspection can proceed even though the operator is not yet hired. Thus by using the "dummy constraint" the network does not show a false dependency relationship between hiring the operator and inspecting the equipment.

In constructing an A-O-A network, activities cannot be placed arbitrarily, as was done with the A-O-N network. Rather, the activities must be connected, using dummies as necessary, such that a separate event is obtained for each unique precedence group.

Another illustrative example of the A-O-A can be introduced as follows:

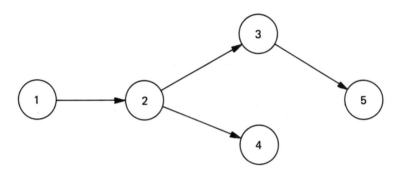

A-O-A Representation of network

To have only one ending node, the network is redrawn as follows:

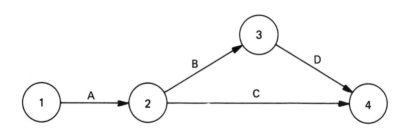

A-O-A conforming to computer-imposed rule no. 3

An A-O-A network viewed by the uninitiated is rarely interpreted correctly. The meaning of dummies and the reason for their presence is not generally obvious. There is also quite often a tendency to confuse the precedence relationships. Dependencies relayed to an event through dummies are subject to being overlooked. Activities originating from a common event are often assumed to be required to start at the same time.

Thus far, the A-O-A system being discussed has been an activity-oriented network. That means that the activities between events were described, and the events were defined only as the completion of all activities leading into them. On some occasions, however, an event-oriented system is employed. This form of the A-O-A system describes the conditions in existence when the event occurs. In this system, an activity, *order materials,* would not be given a description as *materials ordered.* This works fairly well when events have only one activity coming into them, but begins to break down when many activities terminate in the same event. In such a network, it may be impossible for the person unfamiliar with the details of the project to tell what a given activity involves. This system has value when networks are condensed for use by higher management.

COMPARISON OF A-O-N AND A-O-A

Neither network type A-O-N nor A-O-A is based on amount of time required for activities, only on sequence. Neither direction nor path of activities is restricted, although the tendency is to network from left to right. These networks are referred to as "free-body" networks, as opposed to time-scaled networks.

In obtaining the information necessary for the construction of the network (assuming that the network analyst is not the project manager and is not familiar with the project details), the following procedure is recommended.

1. Use the A-O-N system initially.

2. Have the project manager define activities that he or she knows will be involved. Draw a node for each as the information is obtained.

Make no attempt to determine precedence requirements at this time. Continue as long as a project manager can readily think of activities.

3. Connect existing nodes as project manager gives precedence specifications. Additional activities will generally occur to the project manager during this step as they should be added as they are discovered.

Rules for Numbering an A–O–N for Conversion to an A–O–A*

1. Assign two numbers, i and j, to each node. Do not use any number twice. Numbers need not be in any particular order and need not be consecutive. It must be unique. One could then go directly to step 5. Steps 2, 3 and 4 are to eliminate unnecessary dummies from the A-O-A format.

2. If an activity has only one predecessor, change the i number of the activity in question to the j number of the predecessor of the activity in question.

3. If an activity has only one successor, change the j number of the activity in question to the i number of the successor activity—unless doing so would create two activities with the same i-j pair.

4. Apply step 2 to the entire network before applying step 3. Step 3 refers to the numbers existing *after* step 2 has been completed.

5. *For computer input to an A-O-A program,* list each activity with its i-j number. Examine each precedence arrow. If the j number of the activity at the tail of the arrow is not equal to the i number of the activity at the head of the arrow, list the arrow as a dummy activity with its i-j number being the j and i numbers (in that order) listed above. If the j and i numbers mentioned above are equal, do not include any indication of the precedence arrow in the activity list. For drawing the A-O-A network, establish a node (referred to as an event for A-O-A) for each i or j number. Connect with a dashed line those i-j numbers identifying a dummy.

---

*Buchan, Russell J., and Davis, Gordon J. *Project Control Through Network Analysis and Synthesis.* Atlanta: DDR International, 1976 (used with permission).

EXAMPLE OF CONVERSION OF A–O–N TO A–O–A

Equivalent A-O-A Numbers

Act	i	j
A	1	2
B	3	4
C	5	6
D	7	8
E	9	10
F	11	12
Dummy	2	3
,,	2	5
,,	4	7
,,	4	9
,,	6	9
,,	8	11
,,	10	11

Equivalent A-O-A Numbers

Act	i	j
A	1	2
B	2	4
C	2	9
D	4	11
E	9	11
F	11	12
Dummy	4	9

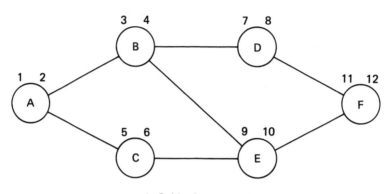

A-O-N after step 1

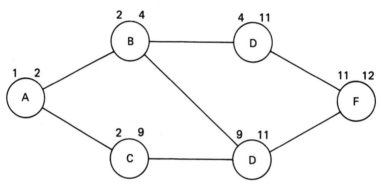

A-O-N after step 4

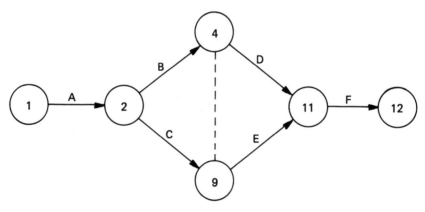

Resulting A-O-A network

C
EVENT-ORIENTED
NETWORK SYSTEMS

Event-oriented systems are basically the activity-on-arrow type, although they have some features of activity-on-node systems. The activities are represented by the arrows, on which time estimates are noted. Activity descriptors, however, are usually written in the past tense and are placed inside the event symbols or nodes.*

An illustrative example can be shown by examining the activity-on-node network as shown in Figure C.1 and reconstruct it for the event-oriented network system as depicted in Figure C.2. An alternative way of showing the last portion of the event-oriented network in Figure C.2, is illustrated in Figure C.3.

In the event systems, the nodes may represent either "start" or "complete" events. To avoid ambiguities at merge and burst points, dummies are often utilized as shown in figures C.2 and C.3, respectively.

ILLUSTRATIVE EXAMPLE

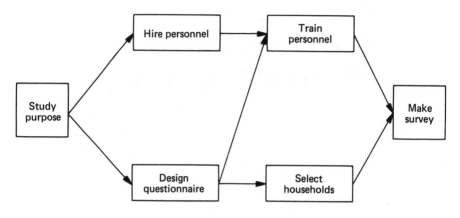

FIGURE C.1 Activity-On-Node Network

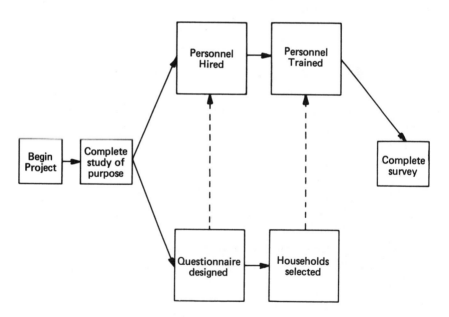

FIGURE C.2 Event-Oriented Network

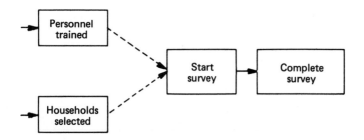

FIGURE C.3 Alternative Way of Showing the Last Portion of the
Event-Oriented Network

COMPARISON OF THE EVENT-ORIENTED SYSTEM WITH THE A-O-N AND A-O-A SYSTEMS

Close comparison of the event-oriented system with the two activity-oriented systems reveals that the event-system is essentially a hybrid of the other two systems.*

*From *Project Management with CPM & PERT* by Joseph Moder and Cecil Phillips. Copyright © 1964 by Van Nostrand Reinhold Company. Reprinted by permission of the publisher.

D
TABLE OF
RANDOM NUMBERS

1368	9621	9151	2066	1208	2664	9822	6599	6911	5112
5953	5936	2541	4011	0408	3593	3679	1378	5936	2651
7226	9466	9553	7671	8599	2119	5337	5953	6355	6889
8883	3454	6773	8207	5576	6386	7487	0190	0867	1298
7022	5281	1168	4099	8069	8721	8353	9952	8006	9045
4576	1853	7884	2451	3488	1286	4842	7719	5795	3953
8715	1416	7028	4616	3470	9938	5703	0196	3465	0034
4011	0408	2224	7626	0643	1149	8834	6429	8691	0143
1400	3694	4482	3608	1238	8221	5129	6105	5314	8385
6370	1884	0820	4854	9161	6509	7123	4070	6759	6113
4522	5749	8084	3932	7678	3549	0051	6761	6952	7041
7195	6234	6426	7148	9945	0358	3242	0519	6550	1327
0054	0810	2937	2040	2299	4198	0846	3937	3986	1019
5166	5433	0381	9686	5670	5129	2103	1125	3404	8785
1247	3793	7415	7819	1783	0506	4878	7673	9840	6629
8529	7842	7203	1844	8619	7404	4215	9969	6948	5643
8973	3440	4366	9242	2151	0244	0922	5887	4883	1177
9307	2959	5904	9012	4951	3695	4529	7197	7179	3239
2923	4276	9467	9868	2257	1925	3382	7244	1781	8037
6372	2808	1238	8098	5509	4617	4099	6705	2386	2830
6922	1807	4900	5306	0411	1828	8634	2331	7247	3230
9862	8336	6453	0545	6127	2741	5967	8447	3017	5709
3371	1530	5104	3076	5506	3101	4143	5845	2095	6127
6712	9402	9588	7019	9248	9192	4223	6555	7947	2474
3071	8782	7157	5941	8830	8563	2252	8109	5880	9912

Random Numbers (cont.)

4022	9734	7852	9096	0051	7387	7056	9331	1317	7833
9682	8892	3577	0326	5306	0050	8517	4376	0788	5443
6705	2175	9904	3743	1902	5393	3032	8432	0612	7972
1872	8292	2366	8603	4288	6809	4357	1072	6822	5611
2559	7534	2281	7351	2064	0611	9613	2000	0327	6145
4399	3751	9783	5399	5175	8894	0296	9483	0400	2272
6074	8827	2195	2532	7680	4288	6807	3101	6850	6410
5155	7186	4722	6721	0838	3632	5355	9369	2006	7681
3193	2800	6184	7891	9838	6123	9397	4019	8389	9508
8610	1880	7423	3384	4625	6653	2900	6290	9286	2396
4778	8818	2992	6300	4239	9595	4384	0611	7687	2088
3987	1619	4164	2542	4042	7799	9084	0278	8422	4330
2977	0248	2793	3351	4922	8878	5703	7421	2054	4391
1312	2919	8220	7285	5902	7882	1403	5354	9913	7109
3890	7193	7799	9190	3275	7840	1872	6232	5295	3148
0793	3468	8762	2492	5854	8430	8472	2264	9279	2128
2139	4552	3444	6462	2524	8601	3372	1848	1472	9667
8277	9153	2880	9053	6880	4284	5044	8931	0861	1517
2236	4778	6639	0862	9509	2141	0208	1450	1222	5281
8837	7686	1771	3374	2894	7314	6856	0440	3766	6047
6605	6380	4599	3333	0713	8401	7146	8940	2629	2006
8399	8175	3525	1646	4019	8390	4344	8975	4489	3423
8053	3046	9102	4515	2944	9763	3003	3408	1199	2791
9837	9378	3237	7016	7593	5958	0068	3114	0456	6840
2557	6395	9496	1884	0612	8102	4402	5498	0422	3335
2604	3074	0504	3828	7881	0797	1094	4098	4940	7067
6930	4180	3074	0060	0909	3187	8991	0682	2385	2307
6160	9899	9084	5704	5666	3051	0325	4733	5905	9226
4884	1857	2847	2581	4870	1782	2980	0587	8797	5545
7294	2009	9020	0006	4309	3941	5645	6238	5052	4150
3478	4973	1056	3687	3145	5988	4214	5543	9185	9375
1764	7860	4150	2881	9895	2531	7363	8756	3724	9359
3025	0890	6436	3461	1411	0303	7422	2684	6256	3495
1771	3056	6630	4982	2386	2517	4747	5505	8785	8708
0254	1892	9066	4890	8716	2258	2452	3913	6790	6331
8537	9966	8224	9151	1855	8911	4422	1913	2000	1482
1475	0261	4465	4803	8231	6469	9935	4256	0648	7768
5209	5569	8410	3041	4325	7290	3381	5209	5571	9458
5456	5944	6038	3210	7165	0723	4820	1846	0005	3865
5043	6694	4853	8425	5871	1322	1052	1452	2486	1669
1719	0148	6977	1244	6443	5955	7945	1218	9391	6485
7432	2955	3933	8110	8585	1893	9218	7153	7566	6040
4926	4761	7812	7439	6436	3145	5934	7852	9095	9497
0769	0683	3768	1048	8519	2987	0124	3064	1881	3177
0805	3139	8514	5014	3274	6395	0549	3858	0820	6406

Random Numbers (cont.)

0204	7273	4964	5475	2648	6977	1371	6971	4850	6873
0092	1733	2349	2648	6609	5676	6445	3271	8867	3469
3139	4867	3666	9783	5088	4852	4143	7923	3858	0504
2033	7430	4389	7121	9982	0651	9110	9731	6421	4731
3921	0530	3605	8455	4205	7363	3081	3931	9331	1313
4111	9244	8135	9877	9529	9160	4407	9077	5306	0054
6573	1570	6654	3616	2049	7001	5185	7108	9270	6550
8515	8029	6880	4329	9367	1087	9549	1684	4838	5686
3590	2106	3245	1989	3529	3828	8091	6054	5656	3035
7212	9909	5005	7660	2620	6406	0690	4240	4070	6549
6701	0154	8806	1716	7029	6776	9465	8818	2886	3547
3777	9532	1333	8131	2929	6987	2408	0487	9172	6177
2495	3054	1692	0089	4090	2983	2136	8947	4625	7177
2073	8878	9742	3012	0042	3996	9930	1651	4982	9645
2252	8004	7840	2105	3033	8749	9153	2872	5100	8674
2104	2224	4052	2273	4753	4505	7156	5417	9725	7599
2371	0005	3844	6654	3246	4853	4301	8886	5217	1153
3270	1214	9649	1872	6930	9791	0248	2687	8126	1501
6209	7237	1966	5541	4224	7080	7630	6422	1160	5675
1309	9126	2920	4359	1726	0562	9654	4182	4097	7493
2406	8013	3634	6428	8091	5925	3923	1686	6097	9670
7365	9859	9378	7084	9402	9201	1815	7064	4324	7081
2889	4738	9929	1476	0785	3832	1281	5821	3690	9185
7951	3781	4755	6986	1659	5727	8108	9816	5759	4188
4548	6778	7672	9101	3911	8127	1918	8512	4197	6402
5701	8342	2852	4278	3343	9830	1756	0546	6717	3114
2187	7266	1210	3797	1636	7917	9933	3518	6923	6349
9360	6640	1315	6284	8265	7232	0291	3467	1088	7834
7850	7626	0745	1992	4998	7349	6451	6186	8916	4292
6186	9233	6571	0925	1748	5490	5264	3820	9829	1335
2671	4690	1550	2262	2597	8034	0785	2978	4409	0237
9111	0250	3275	7519	9740	4577	2064	0286	3398	1348
0391	6035	9230	4999	3332	0608	6113	0391	5789	9926
2475	2144	1886	2079	3004	9686	5669	4367	9306	2595
5336	5845	2095	6446	5694	3641	1085	8705	5416	9066
6808	0423	0155	1652	7897	4335	3567	7109	9690	3739
8525	0577	8940	9451	6726	0876	3818	7607	8854	3566
0398	0741	8787	3043	5063	0617	1770	5048	7721	7032
3623	9636	3638	1406	5731	3978	8068	7238	9715	3363
0739	2644	4917	8866	3632	5399	5175	7422	2476	2607
6713	3041	8133	8749	8835	6745	3597	3476	3816	3455
7775	9315	0432	8327	0861	1515	2297	3375	3713	9174
8599	2122	6842	9202	0810	2936	1514	2090	3067	3574
7955	3759	5254	1126	5553	4713	9605	7909	1658	5490
4766	0070	7260	6033	7997	0109	5993	7592	5436	1727

Random Numbers (cont.)

5165	1670	2534	8811	8231	3721	7947	5719	2640	1394
9111	0513	2751	8256	2931	7783	1281	6531	7259	6993
1667	1084	7889	8963	7018	8617	6381	0723	4926	4551
2145	4587	8585	2412	5431	4667	1942	7238	9613	2212
2739	5528	1481	7528	9368	1823	6979	2547	7268	2467
8769	5480	9160	5354	9700	1362	2774	7980	9157	8788
6531	9435	3422	2474	1475	0159	3414	5224	8399	5820
2937	4134	7120	2206	5084	9473	3958	7320	9878	8609
1581	3285	3727	8924	6204	0797	0882	5945	9375	9153
6268	1045	7076	1436	4165	0143	0293	4190	7171	7932
4293	0523	8625	1961	1039	2856	4889	4358	1492	3804
6936	4213	3212	7229	1230	0019	5998	9206	6753	3762
5334	7641	3258	3769	1362	2771	6124	9813	7915	8960
9373	1158	4418	8826	5665	5896	0358	4717	8232	4859
6968	9428	8950	5346	1741	2348	8143	5377	7695	0685
4229	0587	8794	4009	9691	4579	3302	7673	9629	5246
3807	7785	7097	5701	6639	0723	4819	0900	2713	7650
4891	8829	1642	2155	0796	0466	2946	2970	9143	6590
1055	2968	7911	7479	8199	9735	8271	5339	7058	2964
2983	2345	0568	4125	0894	8302	0506	6761	7706	4310
4026	3129	2968	8053	2797	4022	9838	9611	0975	2437
4075	0260	4256	0337	2355	9371	2954	6021	5783	2827
8488	5450	1327	7358	2034	8060	1788	6913	6123	9405
1976	1749	5742	4098	5887	4567	6064	2777	7830	5668
2793	4701	9466	9554	8294	2160	7486	1557	4769	2781
0916	6272	6825	7188	9611	1181	2301	5516	5451	6832
5961	1149	7946	1950	2010	0600	5655	0796	0569	4365
3222	4189	1891	8172	8731	4769	2782	1325	4238	9279
1176	7834	4600	9992	9449	5824	5344	1008	6678	1921
2369	8971	2314	4806	5071	8908	8274	4936	3357	4441
0041	4329	9265	0352	4764	9070	7527	7791	1094	2008
0803	8302	6814	2422	6351	0637	0514	0246	1845	8594
9965	7804	3930	8803	0268	1426	3130	3613	3947	8086
0011	2387	3148	7559	4216	2946	2865	6333	1916	2259
1767	9871	3914	5790	5287	7915	8959	1346	5482	9251

NOTE: Reprinted with permission from *Handbook of Statistical Tables* by D.B. Owen. Copyright 1962 by Addison-Wesley, Reading, MA, pp. 519–521.

E
COMPUTER APPLICATION
IN PROJECT MANAGEMENT

Because of the number and the routine nature of network calculations, it is desirable to mechanize these calculations for computer computations.

The determination of the earliest start time in a network diagram (see chapter 5) provides an excellent illustration of the way the calculations are automatically carried out by a digitial computer.

Before any computer processing is adopted for critical path calculations, it is necessary that the project manager develop the appropriate network diagram; this diagram must be completed to the stage where each node is numbered and each activity provided with a practical all-normal duration.* If compression investigations are to be made, data must also be prepared for both all-normal and all-crash durations and costs. To facilitate presenting all these data in the format prescribed by the particular computer program or software to be used, most computer companies, like Point 4 Data Corporation, provide a specially prepared write-up to be used for direct input to the 4SITE project control system.

---

*Awani, Alfred O., and Schweikhard W.G. *Planning, Scheduling and Controlling Techniques in Engineering Project Management* (unpublished), Lawrence, KS' University of Kansas, 1980.

4SITE SYSTEM

4SITE is a powerful project control system designed specifically for managers of major multifaceted projects. The 4SITE is an easy to use turnkey system which combines interactive computing capabilities with the advantages of PERT and CPM. It enables the project manager to make decisions in real time, thus enabling him or her to see immediately the effects of his or her decision. By turning raw information into network diagrams, user-defined reports, bar charts, histograms and graphs, the project manager can easily develop and maintain the optimum project plan.

4SITE system is intended for use in aerospace, construction, government, and R & D organizations which control multifaceted projects with PERT/CPM techniques.

READINET PROJECT CONTROL SYSTEM SOFTWARE*

4SITE utilizes POINT 4 Readinet Project Control System Software—the first use of PERT/CPM in an interactive application. Readinet combines interactive computing capabilities with PERT/CPM time, cost, and resources allocation analysis to give a project manager complete control of major multifaceted projects. Its comprehensive real-time program management capability ranges from initial planning to post-project analysis.

Readinet features include:

Entirely interactive

Extensive "what if" capability

Unlimited network size

PERT/CPM and precedence networking features

1260 resources per network plus add-on cost per activity

Tiered subnetworking

Entry of real costs

Manual and automatic resource allocation

*Reprinted by permission from *4SITE Project Management System* by John C. Mather. Copyright by John C. Mather and POINT 4 Data Corporation, Irving, CA.

Networking plotting on any system printer or X-Y plotter

User-defined report generator

Cash flow analysis reports

Change history reports

Electronic notebook

Bar charts, histograms, and graphs

English language inquiry capability

Integrated relational database

Control—From Start to Finish

Using a video terminal, the project manager can:

Develop project plans and schedules

Make projections

Perform cost and resource analysis

Monitor and control updates

Pose "what if" questions

Transform raw information into network diagrams, tabular reports, screen displays, and X-Y plotted graphs

With this start to finish control, a project manager can keep on schedule and within budget.

Input and Output

The input component of the Readinet Project Control System Software as applicable to the Tech Center Project essentially gathers data and prepares it for the computer. In the planning and scheduling stage, data are gathered which identify and describe all the activities necessary for the completion of the project. Next, additional information is established which relates the dependencies of the activities in the Tech Center Project; the Readinet System processes this information and computes: the earliest (ES) and latest (LS) permissible start and the earliest (EF) and latest

(LF) finish times for each activity, identification of the activites on the critical path, the total float, the direct project cost, and total duration for each activity. A calendar project start time (project reference date) as indicated in the program as (1/5/82) and workday schedules (8 hours per day) allow the computer to compute completion dates and resource schedules. Cost information is gathered to develop expenditures which will be used to compare actual expenditures versus planned expenditures. A combination of time, cost, and resource data permits the computer to analyze and develop schedules for labor and equipment.

TECH CENTER PROJECT COMPUTER OUTPUTS

The computer program for the construction of a Tech Center utilizing the Readinet Project Control System Software is presented in succeeding sections.

Section A presents a computer output for the construction of Tech Center. The earliest, latest and total float times for each activity are given; in addition, the critical paths are labeled. The smoothed start (leveled) stresses the minimization of changes in resource levels from one time period to the following.

Section B presents a bar chart by earliest start time of the Tech Center project. The chart is on a time scale. The bar chart is showing complete work, work to be done and float. Note that the critical activities have no float.

Section C presents a cash flow report. This provides the project manager with up-to-date information about expenditures, current and original budget status; variance and also with the total project cost. In addition, figure 15C-1 presents the graph of the actual vs. planned expenditure for the Tech Center Project. The chart is on a time scale with a duration of 52 weeks.

Section D presents a resource histogram, that is, a horizontal bar graph, the length of the bar being proportional to the daily labor situation. From the resource histogram it can be inferred that the available capacity is 20 man-weeks; the line shows this capacity and the underloading. The situation revealed by the histogram is one which is acceptable. For the duration of the project the load did not exceed the capacity, which can have only one result, namely, that activities will take less time than planned, and the overall project time will decrease.

Section E presents the calendar dates for the various months of the Tech Center project with the working day numbered starting from project reference date of January 5, 1982 to the completion of the project, assuming a 5-day work week (Monday through Friday). The calendar dates showed that the Tech Center project was started on January 5, 1982; the material order was placed on day 100 (i.e., May 21, 1982) into the project; the Tech Center project was completed on January 4, 1983 (i.e., 262 working days of project work). From this it is possible to infer that the total duration of the project is 262 working days.

Section F presents the resource allocation for the Tech Center project. This provides the project manager with the opportunity for the day-to-day management decisions. He or she can immediately see the impact of delays and changes in priority. This also provides the project manager with a statement of the total resources required at any one time.

SECTION E (a)

```
- - - R E A D I N E T - - -



POINT 4 DATA CORP
```

```
PROJECT NAME:                   TECH CENTER
PROJECT REFERENCE DATE:         1/5/82
RUN DATE:                       4/ 2/82
TIME:                           8:22
DAYS PER WEEK:                  5
HOURS PER DAY:                  8
```

ACT NO	DESCRIPTION	EARLIEST START	EARLIEST FINISH	LATEST START	LATEST FINISH	TOT FLOAT	CRIT FLAG
1	CALC COST OF ACCESS	1/ 5/82	1/22/82	–	–	–	
2	CALC COST OF SITE W	1/ 5/82	1/25/82	–	–	–	
3	CALC COST OF MATERI	1/ 5/82	1/29/82	–	–	–	
4	PRODUCE BID	1/29/82	4/ 9/82	4/ 2/82	4/ 9/82	0	CRIT
5	BID EVALUATION PERI	4/ 9/82	5/21/82	4/ 9/82	5/21/82	0	CRIT
6	RENT PLANT & EQUIP	5/21/82	6/ 4/82	6/ 4/82	6/18/82	10	
7	HIRE LABOR	5/21/82	6/ 2/82	6/ 8/82	6/18/82	12	
8	ORDER MATERIALS	5/21/82	6/18/82	5/21/82	6/18/82	0	CRIT
9	SURVEY ACCESS ROADS	6/18/82	6/29/82	9/24/82	10/ 5/82	70	
10	SURVEY SITE	6/18/82	7/ 8/82	6/18/82	7/ 8/82	0	CRIT
11	CONSTRUCT ACCESS RO	6/29/82	9/27/82	10/ 5/82	1/ 3/83	70	
12	CLEAR SITE	7/ 8/82	8/ 3/82	7/ 8/82	8/ 3/82	0	CRIT
13	DIG FOOTINGS	8/ 3/82	8/19/82	8/ 3/82	8/19/82	0	CRIT
14	POUR FOOTINGS	8/19/82	8/25/82	8/19/82	8/25/82	0	CRIT
15	DELAY FOR CONCRETE	8/25/82	9/ 8/82	8/25/82	9/ 8/82	0	CRIT
16	CONSTRUCT WALLS	9/ 8/82	10/26/82	9/ 8/82	10/26/82	0	CRIT
17	LANDSCAPE SITE	10/26/82	12/28/82	11/ 1/82	1/ 3/83	4	
18	ERECT ROOF TRUSSES	10/26/82	11/ 4/82	10/26/82	11/ 4/82	0	CRIT
19	FINISH ROOF	11/ 4/82	11/18/82	11/ 4/82	11/18/82	0	CRIT
20	DECORATE INTERIOR	11/18/82	12/14/82	12/ 8/82	1/ 3/83	14	
21	INSTALL FITTINGS	11/18/82	1/ 3/83	11/18/82	1/ 3/83	0	CRIT
22	INSTALL WIRING	10/26/82	11/23/82	12/ 6/82	1/ 3/83	29	
23	INSTALL PLUMBING	10/26/82	12/ 7/82	11/22/82	1/ 3/83	19	
24	INSTALL GAS	10/26/82	12/ 1/82	11/26/82	1/ 3/83	23	
25	INAUGURATE BUILDING	1/ 3/83	1/ 4/83	1/ 3/83	1/ 4/83	0	CRIT

CONDITIONAL CODES: >MASK=ACCESS

ACT NO	DESCRIPTION	EARLIEST FINISH	LATEST FINISH	RES.	ADD-ON COST	LABR	TOT. FLOAT	CRIT FLAG
1	CALC COST OF ACCESS	1/22/82	–	MNGR FMAN ACT	1000.0		–	
9	SURVEY ACCESS ROADS	6/29/82	10/ 5/82	FMAN SRVR LABR	4000.0	2.0	70	
11	CONSTRUCT ACCESS RO	9/27/82	1/ 3/83	FMAN MNGR LABR SRVR ARCH	55000.0	12.0	70	

CONDITIONAL CODES: >CRIT. ACTS

ACT NO	DESCRIPTION	EARLIEST FINISH	LATEST FINISH	ORIG. E.FINISH	ORIG. L.FINISH	SMOOTHED START
4	PRODUCE BID	4/ 9/82	4/ 9/82	3/29/82	3/29/82	4/ 2/82
5	BID EVALUATION PERI	5/21/82	5/21/82	5/10/82	5/10/82	4/ 9/82
8	ORDER MATERIALS	6/18/82	6/18/82	6/ 7/82	6/ 7/82	5/21/82
10	SURVEY SITE	7/ 8/82	7/ 8/82	6/25/82	6/25/82	6/18/82
12	CLEAR SITE	8/ 3/82	8/ 3/82	7/21/82	7/21/82	7/ 8/82
13	DIG FOOTINGS	8/19/82	8/19/82	8/ 6/82	8/ 6/82	8/ 3/82
14	POUR FOOTINGS	8/25/82	8/25/82	8/12/82	8/12/82	8/19/82
15	DELAY FOR CONCRETE	9/ 8/82	9/ 8/82	8/26/82	8/26/82	8/25/82
16	CONSTRUCT WALLS	10/26/82	10/26/82	10/13/82	10/13/82	9/ 8/82
18	ERECT ROOF TRUSSES	11/ 4/82	11/ 4/82	10/22/82	10/22/82	10/26/82
19	FINISH ROOF	'1/18/82	11/18/82	11/ 5/82	11/ 5/82	11/ 4/82
21	INSTALL FITTINGS	1/ 3/83	1/ 3/83	12/21/82	12/21/82	11/18/82
25	INAUGURATE BUILDING	1/ 4/83	1/ 4/83	11/ 8/82	12/21/82	4/20/83

ACT NO	DESCRIPTION	EARLIEST FINISH	LATEST FINISH	ORIG. E.FINISH	ORIG. L.FINISH	SMOOTHED FINISH
1	CALC COST OF ACCESS	1/22/82	–	2/18/82	3/12/82	–
2	CALC COST OF SITE W	1/25/82	–	3/12/82	3/12/82	–
3	CALC COST OF MATERI	1/29/82	–	2/19/82	3/12/82	–
4	PRODUCE BID	4/ 9/82	4/ 9/82	3/29/82	3/29/82	4/ 9/82
5	BID EVALUATION PERI	5/21/82	5/21/82	5/10/82	5/10/82	5/21/82
6	RENT PLANT & EQUIP	6/ 4/82	6/18/82	5/24/82	6/ 7/82	6/ 4/82
7	HIRE LABOR	6/ 2/82	6/18/82	5/20/82	6/ 7/82	6/ 2/82
8	ORDER MATERIALS	6/18/82	6/18/82	6/ 7/82	6/ 7/82	6/18/82
9	SURVEY ACCESS ROADS	6/29/82	10/ 5/82	6/16/82	9/22/82	6/29/82
10	SURVEY SITE	7/ 8/82	7/ 8/82	6/25/82	6/25/82	7/ 8/82
11	CONSTRUCT ACCESS RO	9/27/82	1/ 3/83	9/14/82	12/21/82	2/16/83
12	CLEAR SITE	8/ 3/82	8/ 3/82	7/21/82	7/21/82	8/ 3/82
13	DIG FOOTINGS	8/19/82	8/19/82	8/ 6/82	8/ 6/82	8/19/82
14	POUR FOOTINGS	8/25/82	8/25/82	8/12/82	8/12/82	8/25/82
15	DELAY FOR CONCRETE	9/ 8/82	9/ 8/82	8/26/82	8/26/82	9/ 8/82
16	CONSTRUCT WALLS	10/26/82	10/26/82	10/13/82	10/13/82	10/26/82
17	LANDSCAPE SITE	12/28/82	1/ 3/83	12/15/82	12/21/82	4/20/83
18	ERECT ROOF TRUSSES	11/ 4/82	11/ 4/82	10/22/82	10/22/82	11/ 4/82
19	FINISH ROOF	11/18/82	11/18/82	11/ 5/82	11/ 5/82	11/18/82
20	DECORATE INTERIOR	12/14/82	1/ 3/83	12/ 1/82	12/21/82	1/24/83
21	INSTALL FITTINGS	1/ 3/83	1/ 3/83	12/21/82	12/21/82	1/ 3/83
22	INSTALL WIRING	11/23/82	1/ 3/83	11/10/82	12/21/82	12/29/82
23	INSTALL PLUMBING	12/ 7/82	1/ 3/83	11/24/82	12/21/82	12/ 7/82
24	INSTALL GAS	12/ 1/82	1/ 3/83	11/18/82	12/21/82	12/ 1/82
25	INAUGURATE BUILDING	1/ 4/83	1/ 4/83	11/ 8/82	12/21/82	4/21/83

ACT NO	DESCRIPTION	SMOOTHED START	SMOOTHED FINISH	TOT. FLOAT	SCHED. STATUS	BUDGET STATUS	COMP. STATUS
1	CALC COST OF ACCESS	–	–	–	COMPL.	COMPL.	1/22/82
2	CALC COST OF SITE W	–	–	–	COMPL.	COMPL.	1/25/82
3	CALC COST OF MATERI	–	–	–	COMPL.	COMPL.	1/29/82
4	PRODUCE BID	4/ 2/82	4/ 9/82	0	BEHIND	OVER	50.0%
5	BID EVALUATION PERI	4/ 9/82	5/21/82	0	BEHIND	ON-BDGT	0.0%
6	RENT PLANT & EQUIP	5/21/82	6/ 4/82	10	ON-TIME	OVER	0.0%
7	HIRE LABOR	5/21/82	6/ 2/82	12	ON-TIME	OVER	0.0%
8	ORDER MATERIALS	5/21/82	6/18/82	0	BEHIND	OVER	0.0%
9	SURVEY ACCESS ROADS	6/18/82	6/29/82	70	ON-TIME	OVER	0.0%
10	SURVEY SITE	6/18/82	7/ 8/82	0	BEHIND	OVER	0.0%
11	CONSTRUCT ACCESS RO	11/18/82	2/16/83	70	ON-TIME	OVER	0.0%
12	CLEAR SITE	7/ 8/82	8/ 3/82	0	BEHIND	OVER	0.0%
13	DIG FOOTINGS	8/ 3/82	8/19/82	0	BEHIND	OVER	0.0%
14	POUR FOOTINGS	8/19/82	8/25/82	0	BEHIND	OVER	0.0%
15	DELAY FOR CONCRETE	8/25/82	9/ 8/82	0	BEHIND	ON-BDGT	0.0%
16	CONSTRUCT WALLS	9/ 8/82	10/26/82	0	BEHIND	OVER	0.0%
17	LANDSCAPE SITE	2/16/83	4/20/83	4	BEHIND	OVER	0.0%
18	ERECT ROOF TRUSSES	10/26/82	11/ 4/82	0	BEHIND	OVER	0.0%
19	FINISH ROOF	11/ 4/82	11/18/82	0	BEHIND	OVER	0.0%
20	DECORATE INTERIOR	12/29/82	1/24/83	14	ON-TIME	OVER	0.0%
21	INSTALL FITTINGS	11/18/82	1/ 3/83	0	BEHIND	OVER	0.0%
22	INSTALL WIRING	12/ 1/82	12/29/82	29	ON-TIME	OVER	0.0%
23	INSTALL PLUMBING	10/26/82	12/ 7/82	19	ON-TIME	OVER	0.0%
24	INSTALL GAS	10/26/82	12/ 1/82	23	ON-TIME	OVER	0.0%
25	INAUGURATE BUILDING	4/20/83	4/21/83	0	BEHIND	OVER	0.0%

CONDITIONAL CODES: >CRIT. ACTS

ACT NO	DESCRIPTION	SMOOTHED START	SMOOTHED FINISH	COMP. STATUS	ACTUAL COMPL.	REMARKS
4	PRODUCE BID	4/ 2/82	4/ 9/82	50.0%		
5	BID EVALUATION PERI	4/ 9/82	5/21/82	0.0%		
8	ORDER MATERIALS	5/21/82	6/18/82	0.0%		
10	SURVEY SITE	6/18/82	7/ 8/82	0.0%		
12	CLEAR SITE	7/ 8/82	8/ 3/82	0.0%		
13	DIG FOOTINGS	8/ 3/82	8/19/82	0.0%		
14	POUR FOOTINGS	8/19/82	8/25/82	0.0%		
15	DELAY FOR CONCRETE	8/25/82	9/ 8/82	0.0%		
16	CONSTRUCT WALLS	9/ 8/82	10/26/82	0.0%		
18	ERECT ROOF TRUSSES	10/26/82	11/ 4/82	0.0%		
19	FINISH ROOF	11/ 4/82	11/18/82	0.0%		
21	INSTALL FITTINGS	11/18/82	1/ 3/83	0.0%		
25	INAUGURATE BUILDING	4/20/83	4/21/83	0.0%		

SECTION E (b)

```
                              EVENT REPORT                    SORT OPTION:  2

EVENT      DESCRIPTION                   CODE DATE        E. DATE   L. DATE   CRIT

 10        START OF TECH CENTER          B    1/5/82      1/ 5/82   4/ 1/82
 40        ORDER PLACED                  K                5/21/82   5/21/82   CRIT
160        TECH CENTER COMPLETE          E                1/ 4/83   1/ 4/83   CRIT

                     BAR CHART BY EARLIEST START           1 COL= 11  DAYS


YEAR                       82   82   82   82   82   82   83   83   83   83   83   83
MNTH                        1    3    5    7    9   11    1    3    5    7    9   11
DAY                         4    5    6    7    7    8    7   10   11   12   12   11
ACT   DESCRIPTION          *...*...*...*...*...*...*...*...*...*...*...*
 1    CALC COST OF ACCESS  CC  :^  :    :    :    :    :    :    :    :    :    :
 2    CALC COST OF SITE WO CC  :^  :    :    :    :    :    :    :    :    :    :
 3    CALC COST OF MATERIA CC  :^  :    :    :    :    :    :    :    :    :    :
 4    PRODUCE BID          :CCCC** :    :    :    :    :    :    :    :    :    :
 5    BID EVALUATION PERIO :   :^**** :    :    :    :    :    :    :    :    :
 6    RENT PLANT & EQUIP   :   :^  :** :    :    :    :    :    :    :    :    :
 7    HIRE LABOR           :   :^  :** :    :    :    :    :    :    :    :    :
 8    ORDER MATERIALS      :   :^  :***:    :    :    :    :    :    :    :    :
 9    SURVEY ACCESS ROADS  :   :^  :  **------    :    :    :    :    :    :    :
10    SURVEY SITE          :   :^  :  **-    :    :    :    :    :    :    :    :
11    CONSTRUCT ACCESS ROA :   :^  :  *******------:    :    :    :    :    :
12    CLEAR SITE           :   :^  :  *** :    :    :    :    :    :    :    :
13    DIG FOOTINGS         :   :^  :  :** :    :    :    :    :    :    :    :
14    POUR FOOTINGS        :   :^  :  : *-:    :    :    :    :    :    :    :
15    DELAY FOR CONCRETE T :   :^  :  :  ** :    :    :    :    :    :    :    :
16    CONSTRUCT WALLS      :   :^  :  :  ****:    :    :    :    :    :    :
17    LANDSCAPE SITE       :   :^  :  :    *****:   :    :    :    :    :    :
18    ERECT ROOF TRUSSES   :   :^  :  :    ** :    :    :    :    :    :    :
19    FINISH ROOF          :   :^  :  :    ** :    :    :    :    :    :    :
20    DECORATE INTERIOR    :   :^  :  :    ***-:   :    :    :    :    :    :
21    INSTALL FITTINGS     :   :^  :  :    ****:   :    :    :    :    :    :
22    INSTALL WIRING       :   :^  :  :    ***--:   :    :    :    :    :    :
23    INSTALL PLUMBING     :   :^  :  :    ****-:   :    :    :    :    :    :
24    INSTALL GAS          :   :^  :  :    ***--:   :    :    :    :    :    :
25    INAUGURATE BUILDING  :   :^  :  :    :   *:    :    :    :    :    :    :

          ^ =TIME NOW,  C =COMPLETE,  * =WORK TO BE DONE,  - =FLOAT
```

SECTION E (c)

CASH FLOW REPORT

WEEK	EXPENDITURE	CURRENT BUDGET	ORIGINAL BUDGET	VARIANCE
1/ 4/82	5687.43	0.00	4914.51	-772.91
1/11/82	7962.40	0.00	6143.14	-1819.26
1/18/82	4819.78	0.00	6143.14	1323.36
1/25/82	368.55	0.00	2347.73	1979.17
2/ 1/82	368.55	0.00	1928.66	1560.11
2/ 8/82	368.55	0.00	1928.66	1560.11
2/15/82	368.55	0.00	2924.14	2555.59
2/22/82	368.55	0.00	3173.01	2804.46
3/ 1/82	368.55	0.00	1269.20	900.65
3/ 8/82	368.55	0.00	0.00	-368.55
3/15/82	368.55	0.00	0.00	-368.55
3/22/82	368.55	0.00	0.00	-368.55
3/29/82	263.25	1269.20	0.00	-1532.46 <-
4/ 5/82	0.00	1903.81	0.00	-1903.81
4/12/82	0.00	0.00	4389.60	4389.60
4/19/82	0.00	0.00	7316.00	7316.00
4/26/82	0.00	0.00	3366.80	3366.80
5/ 3/82	0.00	2926.40	2262.00	-664.40
5/10/82	0.00	9784.00	6012.27	-3771.72
5/17/82	0.00	3719.20	8943.30	5224.10
5/24/82	0.00	6917.07	10666.71	3749.64
5/31/82	0.00	9042.27	19577.76	10535.49
6/ 7/82	0.00	11892.01	21805.53	9913.52
6/14/82	0.00	20803.06	21805.53	1002.46
6/21/82	0.00	20803.06	20433.02	-370.03
6/28/82	0.00	12568.02	14943.00	2374.97
7/ 5/82	0.00	16403.12	14943.00	-1460.12
7/12/82	0.00	20420.88	26548.44	6127.56
7/19/82	0.00	2796.72	6946.20	4149.47
7/26/82	0.00	19577.10	6946.20	-12630.90
8/ 2/82	0.00	19577.10	20929.84	1352.74
8/ 9/82	0.00	19577.10	20929.84	1352.74
8/16/82	0.00	19577.10	18151.36	-1425.73
8/23/82	0.00	28890.54	13983.64	-14906.89
8/30/82	0.00	48096.31	13983.64	-34112.67
9/ 6/82	0.00	37901.74	13983.64	-23918.10
9/13/82	0.00	34313.11	21478.04	-12835.07
9/20/82	0.00	31811.43	51455.64	19644.21
9/27/82	0.00	24844.78	43299.99	18455.20
10/ 4/82	0.00	24844.78	41261.07	16416.29
10/11/82	0.00	23636.51	49276.86	25640.34
10/18/82	0.00	20128.37	28666.21	8537.83
10/25/82	0.00	19220.18	21186.65	1966.46
11/ 1/82	0.00	13771.06	17113.34	3342.28
11/ 8/82	0.00	13771.06	13480.60	-290.46
11/15/82	0.00	13814.19	11504.68	-2309.51
11/22/82	0.00	13831.44	2160.60	-11670.84
11/29/82	0.00	13831.44	0.00	-13831.44
12/ 6/82	0.00	13831.44	0.00	-13831.44
12/13/82	0.00	13831.44	0.00	-13831.44
12/20/82	0.00	13831.44	0.00	-13831.44
12/27/82	0.00	25386.00	0.00	-25386.00

CASH FLOW REPORT

WEEK	EXPENDITURE	CURRENT BUDGET	ORIGINAL BUDGET	VARIANCE
TOTALS	22049.86	649144.61	630523.35	-40671.12

TOTAL PROJECT COST: 671194.48

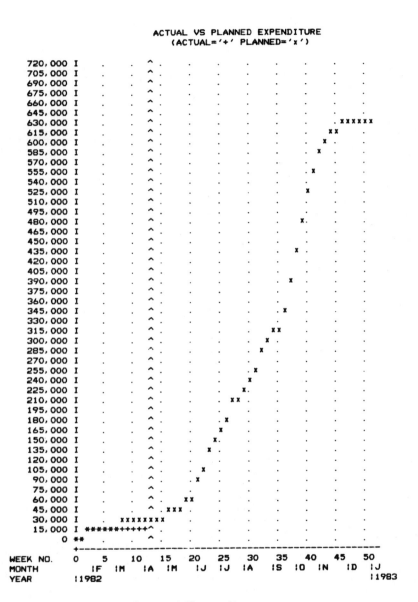

FIGURE E-c.1. Actual vs. Planned Expenditure

SECTION E (d)

```
                                    RESOURCE HISTOGRAM        RESOURCE: LABR
            5     10    15    20    25    30    35    40    45   50    55
        . . . . *. . . . *. . . . *. . . . *. . . . *. . . . *. . . . *. . . . *. . . . *. . . . *. . . . *

4/ 2/82                           ^                                         0. 0

4/ 5/82                           ^                                         0. 0
4/ 6/82                           ^                                         0. 0
4/ 7/82                           ^                                         0. 0
4/ 8/82                           ^                                         0. 0
4/ 9/82                           ^                                         0. 0

4/12/82                           ^                                         0. 0
4/13/82                           ^                                         0. 0
4/14/82                           ^                                         0. 0
4/15/82                           ^                                         0. 0
4/16/82                           ^                                         0. 0

4/19/82                           ^                                         0. 0
4/20/82                           ^                                         0. 0
4/21/82                           ^                                         0. 0
4/22/82                           ^                                         0. 0
4/23/82                           ^                                         0. 0

4/26/82                           ^                                         0. 0
4/27/82                           ^                                         0. 0
4/28/82                           ^                                         0. 0
4/29/82                           ^                                         0. 0
4/30/82                           ^                                         0. 0

5/ 3/82                           ^                                         0. 0
5/ 4/82                           ^                                         0. 0
5/ 5/82                           ^                                         0. 0
5/ 6/82                           ^                                         0. 0
5/ 7/82                           ^                                         0. 0

5/10/82                           ^                                         0. 0
5/11/82                           ^                                         0. 0
5/12/82                           ^                                         0. 0
5/13/82                           ^                                         0. 0
5/14/82                           ^                                         0. 0

5/17/82                           ^                                         0. 0
5/18/82                           ^                                         0. 0
5/19/82                           ^                                         0. 0
5/20/82                           ^                                         0. 0
5/21/82                           ^                                         0. 0

5/24/82                           ^                                         0. 0
5/25/82                           ^                                         0. 0
5/26/82                           ^                                         0. 0
5/27/82                           ^                                         0. 0
5/28/82                           ^                                         0. 0
```

```
                                   RESOURCE HISTOGRAM           RESOURCE: LABR
              5     10    15    20    25    30    35    40    45    50    55
         . . . .*. . . .*. . . .*. . . .*. . . .*. . . .*. . . .*. . . .*. . . .*. . . .*. . . .*

5/31/82                            ^                                          0. 0
6/ 1/82                            ^                                          0. 0
6/ 2/82                            ^                                          0. 0
6/ 3/82                            ^                                          0. 0
6/ 4/82                            ^                                          0. 0

6/ 7/82                            ^                                          0. 0
6/ 8/82                            ^                                          0. 0
6/ 9/82                            ^                                          0. 0
6/10/82                            ^                                          0. 0
6/11/82                            ^                                          0. 0

6/14/82                            ^                                          0. 0
6/15/82                            ^                                          0. 0
6/16/82                            ^                                          0. 0
6/17/82                            ^                                          0. 0
6/18/82   ****                     ^                                          4. 0

6/21/82   ****                     ^                                          4. 0
6/22/82   ****                     ^                                          4. 0
6/23/82   ****                     ^                                          4. 0
6/24/82   ****                     ^                                          4. 0
6/25/82   ****                     ^                                          4. 0

6/28/82   ****                     ^                                          4. 0
6/29/82   **                       ^                                          2. 0
6/30/82   **                       ^                                          2. 0
7/ 1/82   **                       ^                                          2. 0
7/ 2/82   **                       ^                                          2. 0

7/ 5/82   **                       ^                                          2. 0
7/ 6/82   **                       ^                                          2. 0
7/ 7/82   **                       ^                                          2. 0
7/ 8/82   ************             ^                                          12. 0
7/ 9/82   ************             ^                                          12. 0

7/12/82   ************             ^                                          12. 0
7/13/82   ************             ^                                          12. 0
7/14/82   ************             ^                                          12. 0
7/15/82   ************             ^                                          12. 0
7/16/82   ************             ^                                          12. 0

7/19/82   ************             ^                                          12. 0
7/20/82   ************             ^                                          12. 0
7/21/82   ************             ^                                          12. 0
7/22/82   ************             ^                                          12. 0
7/23/82   ************             ^                                          12. 0

7/26/82   ************             ^                                          12. 0
7/27/82   ************             ^                                          12. 0
7/28/82   ************             ^                                          12. 0
7/29/82   ************             ^                                          12. 0
7/30/82   ************             ^                                          12. 0
```

```
                                   RESOURCE HISTOGRAM              RESOURCE: LABR
                    5    10   15   20   25   30   35   40   45   50   55
                 ....*....*....*....*....*....*....*....*....*....*....*

8/ 2/82   ************            ^                                        12. 0
8/ 3/82   ********               ^                                         8. 0
8/ 4/82   ********               ^                                         8. 0
8/ 5/82   ********               ^                                         8. 0
8/ 6/82   ********               ^                                         8. 0

8/ 9/82   ********               ^                                         8. 0
8/10/82   ********               ^                                         8. 0
8/11/82   ********               ^                                         8. 0
8/12/82   ********               ^                                         8. 0
8/13/82   ********               ^                                         8. 0

8/16/82   ********               ^                                         8. 0
8/17/82   ********               ^                                         8. 0
8/18/82   ********               ^                                         8. 0
8/19/82   **************         ^                                         14. 0
8/20/82   **************         ^                                         14. 0

8/23/82   **************         ^                                         14. 0
8/24/82   **************         ^                                         14. 0
8/25/82                          ^                                         0. 0
8/26/82                          ^                                         0. 0
8/27/82                          ^                                         0. 0

8/30/82                          ^                                         0. 0
8/31/82                          ^                                         0. 0
9/ 1/82                          ^                                         0. 0
9/ 2/82                          ^                                         0. 0
9/ 3/82                          ^                                         0. 0

9/ 6/82                          ^                                         0. 0
9/ 7/82                          ^                                         0. 0
9/ 8/82   **********             ^                                         10. 0
9/ 9/82   **********             ^                                         10. 0
9/10/82   **********             ^                                         10. 0

9/13/82   **********             ^                                         10. 0
9/14/82   **********             ^                                         10. 0
9/15/82   **********             ^                                         10. 0
9/16/82   **********             ^                                         10. 0
9/17/82   **********             ^                                         10. 0

9/20/82   **********             ^                                         10. 0
9/21/82   **********             ^                                         10. 0
9/22/82   **********             ^                                         10. 0
9/23/82   **********             ^                                         10. 0
9/24/82   **********             ^                                         10. 0

9/27/82   **********             ^                                         10. 0
9/28/82   **********             ^                                         10. 0
9/29/82   **********             ^                                         10. 0
9/30/82   **********             ^                                         10. 0
10/ 1/82  **********             ^                                         10. 0
```

```
                                   RESOURCE HISTOGRAM          RESOURCE: LABR
              5    10   15   20   25   30   35   40   45   50   55
           ....*....*....*....*....*....*....*....*....*....*....*

10/ 4/82   **********           ^                                        10.0
10/ 5/82   **********           ^                                        10.0
10/ 6/82   **********           ^                                        10.0
10/ 7/82   **********           ^                                        10.0
10/ 8/82   **********           ^                                        10.0

10/11/82   **********           ^                                        10.0
10/12/82   **********           ^                                        10.0
10/13/82   **********           ^                                        10.0
10/14/82   **********           ^                                        10.0
10/15/82   **********           ^                                        10.0

10/18/82   **********           ^                                        10.0
10/19/82   **********           ^                                        10.0
10/20/82   **********           ^                                        10.0
10/21/82   **********           ^                                        10.0
10/22/82   **********           ^                                        10.0

10/25/82   **********           ^                                        10.0
10/26/82   *************        ^                                        13.0
10/27/82   *************        ^                                        13.0
10/28/82   *************        ^                                        13.0
10/29/82   *************        ^                                        13.0

11/ 1/82   *************        ^                                        13.0
11/ 2/82   *************        ^                                        13.0
11/ 3/82   *************        ^                                        13.0
11/ 4/82   *************        ^                                        13.0
11/ 5/82   *************        ^                                        13.0

11/ 8/82   *************        ^                                        13.0
11/ 9/82   *************        ^                                        13.0
11/10/82   *************        ^                                        13.0
11/11/82   *************        ^                                        13.0
11/12/82   *************        ^                                        13.0

11/15/82   *************        ^                                        13.0
11/16/82   *************        ^                                        13.0
11/17/82   *************        ^                                        13.0
11/18/82   *******************^                                          20.0
11/19/82   *******************^                                          20.0

11/22/82   *******************^                                          20.0
11/23/82   *******************^                                          20.0
11/24/82   *******************^                                          20.0
11/25/82   *******************^                                          20.0
11/26/82   *******************^                                          20.0

11/29/82   *******************^                                          20.0
11/30/82   *******************^                                          20.0
12/ 1/82   *******************^                                          19.0
12/ 2/82   *******************^                                          19.0
12/ 3/82   *******************^                                          19.0
```

```
                              RESOURCE HISTOGRAM        RESOURCE: LABR
                 5    10   15   20   25   30   35   40   45   50   55
               ...*....*....*....*....*....*....*....*....*....*....*

12/ 6/82    ********************^                                      19.0
12/ 7/82    ******************* ^                                      18.0
12/ 8/82    ****************** ^                                       18.0
12/ 9/82    ****************** ^                                       18.0
12/10/82    ****************** ^                                       18.0

12/13/82    ****************** ^                                       18.0
12/14/82    ****************** ^                                       18.0
12/15/82    ****************** ^                                       18.0
12/16/82    ****************** ^                                       18.0
12/17/82    ****************** ^                                       18.0

12/20/82    ****************** ^                                       18.0
12/21/82    ****************** ^                                       18.0
12/22/82    ****************** ^                                       18.0
12/23/82    ****************** ^                                       18.0
12/24/82    ****************** ^                                       18.0

12/27/82    ****************** ^                                       18.0
12/28/82    ****************** ^                                       18.0
12/29/82    ********************^                                      20.0
12/30/82    ********************^                                      20.0
12/31/82    ********************^                                      20.0

1/ 3/83     ***************       ^                                    15.0
1/ 4/83     ***************       ^                                    15.0
1/ 5/83     ***************       ^                                    15.0
1/ 6/83     ***************       ^                                    15.0
1/ 7/83     ***************       ^                                    15.0

1/10/83     ***************       ^                                    15.0
1/11/83     ***************       ^                                    15.0
1/12/83     ***************       ^                                    15.0
1/13/83     ***************       ^                                    15.0
1/14/83     ***************       ^                                    15.0

1/17/83     ***************       ^                                    15.0
1/18/83     ***************       ^                                    15.0
1/19/83     ***************       ^                                    15.0
1/20/83     ***************       ^                                    15.0
1/21/83     ***************       ^                                    15.0

1/24/83     ************         ^                                     12.0
1/25/83     ************         ^                                     12.0
1/26/83     ************         ^                                     12.0
1/27/83     ************         ^                                     12.0
1/28/83     ************         ^                                     12.0

1/31/83     ************         ^                                     12.0
2/ 1/83     ************         ^                                     12.0
2/ 2/83     ************         ^                                     12.0
2/ 3/83     ************         ^                                     12.0
2/ 4/83     ************         ^                                     12.0

                              RESOURCE HISTOGRAM        RESOURCE: LABR
                 5    10   15   20   25   30   35   40   45   50   55
               ...*....*....*....*....*....*....*....*....*....*....*

2/ 7/83     ************       ^                                       12.0
2/ 8/83     ************       ^                                       12.0
2/ 9/83     ************       ^                                       12.0
2/10/83     ************       ^                                       12.0
2/11/83     ************       ^                                       12.0
```

2/14/83	************	^	12. 0
2/15/83	************	^	12. 0
2/16/83	**********	^	10. 0
2/17/83	**********	^	10. 0
2/18/83	**********	^	10. 0
2/21/83	**********	^	10. 0
2/22/83	**********	^	10. 0
2/23/83	**********	^	10. 0
2/24/83	**********	^	10. 0
2/25/83	**********	^	10. 0
2/28/83	**********	^	10. 0
3/ 1/83	**********	^	10. 0
3/ 2/83	**********	^	10. 0
3/ 3/83	**********	^	10. 0
3/ 4/83	**********	^	10. 0
3/ 7/83	**********	^	10. 0
3/ 8/83	**********	^	10. 0
3/ 9/83	**********	^	10. 0
3/10/83	**********	^	10. 0
3/11/83	**********	^	10. 0
3/14/83	**********	^	10. 0
3/15/83	**********	^	10. 0
3/16/83	**********	^	10. 0
3/17/83	**********	^	10. 0
3/18/83	**********	^	10. 0
3/21/83	**********	^	10. 0
3/22/83	**********	^	10. 0
3/23/83	**********	^	10. 0
3/24/83	**********	^	10. 0
3/25/83	**********	^	10. 0
3/28/83	**********	^	10. 0
3/29/83	**********	^	10. 0
3/30/83	**********	^	10. 0
3/31/83	**********	^	10. 0
4/ 1/83	**********	^	10. 0
4/ 4/83	**********	^	10. 0
4/ 5/83	**********	^	10. 0
4/ 6/83	**********	^	10. 0
4/ 7/83	**********	^	10. 0
4/ 8/83	**********	^	10. 0

```
                        RESOURCE HISTOGRAM          RESOURCE: LABR
        5    10    15    20    25    30    35    40    45    50    55
   ....*....*....*....*....*....*....*....*....*....*....*
```

4/11/83	**********	^	10. 0
4/12/83	**********	^	10. 0
4/13/83	**********	^	10. 0
4/14/83	**********	^	10. 0
4/15/83	**********	^	10. 0
4/18/83	**********	^	10. 0
4/19/83	**********	^	10. 0

SECTION E (e)

```
                                    J A N U A R Y                              1982
        +----------+----------+----------+----------+----------+----------+----------+
        I   SUN    I   MON    I   TUE    I   WED    I   THU    I   FRI    I   SAT    I
        +----------+----------+----------+----------+----------+----------+----------+
DATE    I          I    4     I    5     I    6     I    7     I    8     I          I
DAY NO  I          I    1     I    2     I    3     I    4     I    5     I          I
EVENT   I          I   **     I   **     I          I          I          I          I
        +----------+----------+----------+----------+----------+----------+----------+
DATE    I          I   11     I   12     I   13     I   14     I   15     I          I
DAY NO  I          I    6     I    7     I    8     I    9     I   10     I          I
EVENT   I          I          I          I          I          I          I          I
        +----------+----------+----------+----------+----------+----------+----------+
DATE    I          I   18     I   19     I   20     I   21     I   22     I          I
DAY NO  I          I   11     I   12     I   13     I   14     I   15     I          I
EVENT   I          I          I          I          I          I          I          I
        +----------+----------+----------+----------+----------+----------+----------+
DATE    I          I   25     I   26     I   27     I   28     I   29     I          I
DAY NO  I          I   16     I   17     I   18     I   19     I   20     I          I
EVENT   I          I          I          I          I          I          I          I
        +----------+----------+----------+----------+----------+----------+----------+
                            E V E N T    L I S T
                            =====================
```

```
   1/ 4/82              0          E        TECH CENTER COMPLETE
   1/ 5/82             10          B        START OF TECH CENTER
```

```
                                    F E B R U A R Y                            1982
        +----------+----------+----------+----------+----------+----------+----------+
        I   SUN    I   MON    I   TUE    I   WED    I   THU    I   FRI    I   SAT    I
        +----------+----------+----------+----------+----------+----------+----------+
DATE    I          I    1     I    2     I    3     I    4     I    5     I          I
DAY NO  I          I   21     I   22     I   23     I   24     I   25     I          I
EVENT   I          I          I          I          I          I          I          I
        +----------+----------+----------+----------+----------+----------+----------+
DATE    I          I    8     I    9     I   10     I   11     I   12     I          I
DAY NO  I          I   26     I   27     I   28     I   29     I   30     I          I
EVENT   I          I          I          I          I          I          I          I
        +----------+----------+----------+----------+----------+----------+----------+
DATE    I          I   15     I   16     I   17     I   18     I   19     I          I
DAY NO  I          I   31     I   32     I   33     I   34     I   35     I          I
EVENT   I          I          I          I          I          I          I          I
        +----------+----------+----------+----------+----------+----------+----------+
DATE    I          I   22     I   23     I   24     I   25     I   26     I          I
DAY NO  I          I   36     I   37     I   38     I   39     I   40     I          I
EVENT   I          I          I          I          I          I          I          I
        +----------+----------+----------+----------+----------+----------+----------+
```

M A R C H   1982

	SUN	MON	TUE	WED	THU	FRI	SAT
DATE		1	2	3	4	5	
DAY NO		41	42	43	44	45	
EVENT							
DATE		8	9	10	11	12	
DAY NO		46	47	48	49	50	
EVENT							
DATE		15	16	17	18	19	
DAY NO		51	52	53	54	55	
EVENT							
DATE		22	23	24	25	26	
DAY NO		56	57	58	59	60	
EVENT							
DATE		29	30	31			
DAY NO		61	62	63			
EVENT							

A P R I L   1982

	SUN	MON	TUE	WED	THU	FRI	SAT
DATE					1	2	
DAY NO					64	65	
EVENT							
DATE		5	6	7	8	9	
DAY NO		66	67	68	69	70	
EVENT							
DATE		12	13	14	15	16	
DAY NO		71	72	73	74	75	
EVENT							
DATE		19	20	21	22	23	
DAY NO		76	77	78	79	80	
EVENT							
DATE		26	27	28	29	30	
DAY NO		81	82	83	84	85	
EVENT							

```
                                        M A Y                                    1982
        +---------+---------+---------+---------+---------+---------+---------+
        I   SUN   I   MON   I   TUE   I   WED   I   THU   I   FRI   I   SAT   I
        +---------+---------+---------+---------+---------+---------+---------+
DATE    I         I     3   I     4   I     5   I     6   I     7   I         I
DAY NO  I         I    86   I    87   I    88   I    89   I    90   I         I
EVENT   I         I         I         I         I         I         I         I
        +---------+---------+---------+---------+---------+---------+---------+
DATE    I         I    10   I    11   I    12   I    13   I    14   I         I
DAY NO  I         I    91   I    92   I    93   I    94   I    95   I         I
EVENT   I         I         I         I         I         I         I         I
        +---------+---------+---------+---------+---------+---------+---------+
DATE    I         I    17   I    18   I    19   I    20   I    21   I         I
DAY NO  I         I    96   I    97   I    98   I    99   I   100   I         I
EVENT   I         I         I         I         I         I    **   I         I
        +---------+---------+---------+---------+---------+---------+---------+
DATE    I         I    24   I    25   I    26   I    27   I    28   I         I
DAY NO  I         I   101   I   102   I   103   I   104   I   105   I         I
EVENT   I         I         I         I         I         I         I         I
        +---------+---------+---------+---------+---------+---------+---------+
DATE    I         I    31   I         I         I         I         I         I
DAY NO  I         I   106   I         I         I         I         I         I
EVENT   I         I         I         I         I         I         I         I
        +---------+---------+---------+---------+---------+---------+---------+
                            E V E N T    L I S T
                            =====================

    5/21/82              40        K          ORDER PLACED
```

```
                                        J U N E                                  1982
        +---------+---------+---------+---------+---------+---------+---------+
        I   SUN   I   MON   I   TUE   I   WED   I   THU   I   FRI   I   SAT   I
        +---------+---------+---------+---------+---------+---------+---------+
DATE    I         I         I     1   I     2   I     3   I     4   I         I
DAY NO  I         I         I   107   I   108   I   109   I   110   I         I
EVENT   I         I         I         I         I         I         I         I
        +---------+---------+---------+---------+---------+---------+---------+
DATE    I         I     7   I     8   I     9   I    10   I    11   I         I
DAY NO  I         I   111   I   112   I   113   I   114   I   115   I         I
EVENT   I         I         I         I         I         I         I         I
        +---------+---------+---------+---------+---------+---------+---------+
DATE    I         I    14   I    15   I    16   I    17   I    18   I         I
DAY NO  I         I   116   I   117   I   118   I   119   I   120   I         I
EVENT   I         I         I         I         I         I         I         I
        +---------+---------+---------+---------+---------+---------+---------+
DATE    I         I    21   I    22   I    23   I    24   I    25   I         I
DAY NO  I         I   121   I   122   I   123   I   124   I   125   I         I
EVENT   I         I         I         I         I         I         I         I
        +---------+---------+---------+---------+---------+---------+---------+
DATE    I         I    28   I    29   I    30   I         I         I         I
DAY NO  I         I   126   I   127   I   128   I         I         I         I
EVENT   I         I         I         I         I         I         I         I
        +---------+---------+---------+---------+---------+---------+---------+
```

J U L Y   1982

	SUN	MON	TUE	WED	THU	FRI	SAT
DATE					1	2	
DAY NO					129	130	
EVENT							
DATE		5	6	7	8	9	
DAY NO		131	132	133	134	135	
EVENT							
DATE		12	13	14	15	16	
DAY NO		136	137	138	139	140	
EVENT							
DATE		19	20	21	22	23	
DAY NO		141	142	143	144	145	
EVENT							
DATE		26	27	28	29	30	
DAY NO		146	147	148	149	150	
EVENT							

A U G U S T   1982

	SUN	MON	TUE	WED	THU	FRI	SAT
DATE		2	3	4	5	6	
DAY NO		151	152	153	154	155	
EVENT							
DATE		9	10	11	12	13	
DAY NO		156	157	158	159	160	
EVENT							
DATE		16	17	18	19	20	
DAY NO		161	162	163	164	165	
EVENT							
DATE		23	24	25	26	27	
DAY NO		166	167	168	169	170	
EVENT							
DATE		30	31				
DAY NO		171	172				
EVENT							

S E P T E M B E R   1982

	SUN	MON	TUE	WED	THU	FRI	SAT
DATE				1	2	3	
DAY NO				173	174	175	
EVENT							
DATE		6	7	8	9	10	
DAY NO		176	177	178	179	180	
EVENT							
DATE		13	14	15	16	17	
DAY NO		181	182	183	184	185	
EVENT							
DATE		20	21	22	23	24	
DAY NO		186	187	188	189	190	
EVENT							
DATE		27	28	29	30		
DAY NO		191	192	193	194		
EVENT							

O C T O B E R   1982

	SUN	MON	TUE	WED	THU	FRI	SAT
DATE						1	
DAY NO						195	
EVENT							
DATE		4	5	6	7	8	
DAY NO		196	197	198	199	200	
EVENT							
DATE		11	12	13	14	15	
DAY NO		201	202	203	204	205	
EVENT							
DATE		18	19	20	21	22	
DAY NO		206	207	208	209	210	
EVENT							
DATE		25	26	27	28	29	
DAY NO		211	212	213	214	215	
EVENT							

```
                           N O V E M B E R                        1982

      +----------+----------+----------+----------+----------+----------+----------+
      I   SUN    I   MON    I   TUE    I   WED    I   THU    I   FRI    I   SAT    I
      +----------+----------+----------+----------+----------+----------+----------+
DATE  I          I    1     I    2     I    3     I    4     I    5     I          I
DAY NO I          I  216    I  217    I  218    I  219    I  220    I          I
EVENT I          I          I          I          I          I          I          I
      +----------+----------+----------+----------+----------+----------+----------+
DATE  I          I    8     I    9     I   10     I   11     I   12     I          I
DAY NO I          I  221    I  222    I  223    I  224    I  225    I          I
EVENT I          I          I          I          I          I          I          I
      +----------+----------+----------+----------+----------+----------+----------+
DATE  I          I   15     I   16     I   17     I   18     I   19     I          I
DAY NO I          I  226    I  227    I  228    I  229    I  230    I          I
EVENT I          I          I          I          I          I          I          I
      +----------+----------+----------+----------+----------+----------+----------+
DATE  I          I   22     I   23     I   24     I   25     I   26     I          I
DAY NO I          I  231    I  232    I  233    I  234    I  235    I          I
EVENT I          I          I          I          I          I          I          I
      +----------+----------+----------+----------+----------+----------+----------+
DATE  I          I   29     I   30     I          I          I          I          I
DAY NO I          I  236    I  237    I          I          I          I          I
EVENT I          I          I          I          I          I          I          I
      +----------+----------+----------+----------+----------+----------+----------+
```

```
                           D E C E M B E R                        1982

      +----------+----------+----------+----------+----------+----------+----------+
      I   SUN    I   MON    I   TUE    I   WED    I   THU    I   FRI    I   SAT    I
      +----------+----------+----------+----------+----------+----------+----------+
DATE  I          I          I          I    1     I    2     I    3     I          I
DAY NO I          I          I          I  238    I  239    I  240    I          I
EVENT I          I          I          I          I          I          I          I
      +----------+----------+----------+----------+----------+----------+----------+
DATE  I          I    6     I    7     I    8     I    9     I   10     I          I
DAY NO I          I  241    I  242    I  243    I  244    I  245    I          I
EVENT I          I          I          I          I          I          I          I
      +----------+----------+----------+----------+----------+----------+----------+
DATE  I          I   13     I   14     I   15     I   16     I   17     I          I
DAY NO I          I  246    I  247    I  248    I  249    I  250    I          I
EVENT I          I          I          I          I          I          I          I
      +----------+----------+----------+----------+----------+----------+----------+
DATE  I          I   20     I   21     I   22     I   23     I   24     I          I
DAY NO I          I  251    I  252    I  253    I  254    I  255    I          I
EVENT I          I          I          I          I          I          I          I
      +----------+----------+----------+----------+----------+----------+----------+
DATE  I          I   27     I   28     I   29     I   30     I   31     I          I
DAY NO I          I  256    I  257    I  258    I  259    I  260    I          I
EVENT I          I          I          I          I          I          I          I
      +----------+----------+----------+----------+----------+----------+----------+
```

```
                                  J A N U A R Y                                    1983
         +---------+---------+---------+---------+---------+---------+---------+
         I   SUN   I   MON   I   TUE   I   WED   I   THU   I   FRI   I   SAT   I
         +---------+---------+---------+---------+---------+---------+---------+
DATE     I         I    3    I    4    I    5    I    6    I    7    I         I
DAY NO   I         I   261   I   262   I   263   I   264   I   265   I         I
EVENT    I         I         I   **    I         I         I         I         I
         +---------+---------+---------+---------+---------+---------+---------+
DATE     I         I   10    I   11    I   12    I   13    I   14    I         I
DAY NO   I         I   266   I   267   I   268   I   269   I   270   I         I
EVENT    I         I         I         I         I         I         I         I
         +---------+---------+---------+---------+---------+---------+---------+
DATE     I         I   17    I   18    I   19    I   20    I   21    I         I
DAY NO   I         I   271   I   272   I   273   I   274   I   275   I         I
EVENT    I         I         I         I         I         I         I         I
         +---------+---------+---------+---------+---------+---------+---------+
DATE     I         I   24    I   25    I   26    I   27    I   28    I         I
DAY NO   I         I   276   I   277   I   278   I   279   I   280   I         I
EVENT    I         I         I         I         I         I         I         I
         +---------+---------+---------+---------+---------+---------+---------+
DATE     I         I   31    I         I         I         I         I         I
DAY NO   I         I   281   I         I         I         I         I         I
EVENT    I         I         I         I         I         I         I         I
         +---------+---------+---------+---------+---------+---------+---------+
                            E V E N T    L I S T
                            =====================

   1/ 4/83              160       E        TECH CENTER COMPLETE
```

SECTION E (f)

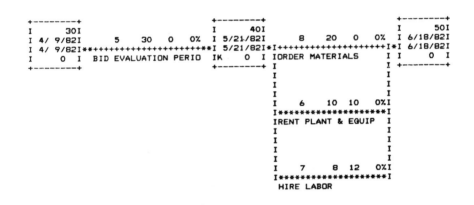

```
+--------+                      +--------+                                    +--------+
I     10I                      I     20I                                     I     30I
I 1/ 5/82I               1    14 COMPLETE  I 1/29/82I      4    11    0   50%  I 4/ 9/82I
I 4/ 2/82I*I+++++++++++++++++++++I*I 4/ 2/82I**++++++++++++++++++++++++++**I 4/ 9/82I
IB   63 I  ICALC COST OF ACCESS I I    45  I  PRODUCE BID                     I    0 I
+--------+  I                   I +--------+                                  +--------+
            I                   I
            I                   I
            I                   I
            I     2    30 COMPLETEI
            I********************I
            ICALC COST OF SITE WOI
            I                   I
            I                   I
            I                   I
            I     3    15 COMPLETEI
            I********************I
             CALC COST OF MATERIA
```

```
+--------+                      +--------+                                    +--------+
I     30I                      I     40I                                     I     50I
I 4/ 9/82I          5    30   0   0%  I 5/21/82I      8    20    0   0%  I 6/18/82I
I 4/ 9/82I**++++++++++++++++++++++**I 5/21/82I*I++++++++++++++++++++++I*I 6/18/82I
I    0 I  BID EVALUATION PERIO  IK    0 I  IORDER MATERIALS        I I    0 I
+--------+                      +--------+  I                       I +--------+
                                            I                       I
                                            I                       I
                                            I                       I
                                            I     6    10  10   0%I
                                            I********************I
                                            IRENT PLANT & EQUIP    I
                                            I                       I
                                            I                       I
                                            I                       I
                                            I     7     8  12   0%I
                                            I********************I
                                             HIRE LABOR
```

```
+--------+                              +--------+                              +--------+
I     50I          10     14    0    0% I     70I          12     18    0    0% I     80I
I 6/18/82I*I+++++++++++++++++++++++++*I 7/ 8/82I**+++++++++++++++++++++++++*I 8/ 3/82I
I 6/18/82I*I+++++++++++++++++++++++++*I 7/ 8/82I**+++++++++++++++++++++++++*I 8/ 3/82I
I    0  I ISURVEY SITE                 I    0  I  CLEAR SITE                 I    0  I
+--------+ I                           +--------+                              +--------+
           I
           I
           I
           I
           I
           I
           I
           I
           I
           I
           I
           I
           I
           I
           I
           I
           I
           I
           I
           I
           I
           I
           I
           I
           I
           I
           I
           I
           I
           I
           I                           +--------+
           I     9    7   70   0%      I     60I          11    64   70   0%
           I*********************I10/ 5/82I********************************
              SURVEY ACCESS ROADS      I    70 I  CONSTRUCT ACCESS ROADS
                                       +--------+
```

```
+--------+                          +--------+                          +--------+
I     80I                           I     90I                           I    100I
I 8/ 3/82I    13    12    0    0%   I 8/19/82I    14    4    0    0%    I 8/25/82I
I 8/ 3/82I*++++++++++++++++++++++**I 8/19/82I*++++++++++++++++++++++**I 8/25/82I
I    0  I  DIG FOOTINGS             I    0  I  POUR FOOTINGS            I    0  I
+--------+                          +--------+                          +--------+




                11    64   70    0%
*********************************************************************************
            CONSTRUCT ACCESS ROADS
```

```
+---------+                               +---------+                               +---------+
I     100I                               I     110I                               I     120I
I 8/25/82I    15     10     0     0%  I 9/ 8/82I    16     34     0     0%  I10/26/82I
I 8/25/82I**++++++++++++++++++++++**I 9/ 8/82I**++++++++++++++++++++++**I10/26/82I
I     0   I  DELAY FOR CONCRETE T  I     0   I  CONSTRUCT WALLS          I     0   I
+---------+                               +---------+                               +---------+




                        11    64    70    0%
*****************************************************************************************
                    CONSTRUCT ACCESS ROADS
```

```
+--------+                          +--------+                          +--------+
I    120I                          I    130I                          I    140I
I10/26/82I    18    7    0    0%  I11/ 4/82I    19   10    0    0%  I11/18/82I
I10/26/82I*I++++++++++++++++++++**I11/ 4/82I**++++++++++++++++++++**I11/18/82I
I    0  I IERECT ROOF TRUSSES     1    0  I FINISH ROOF               I    0  I
+--------+ I                        +--------+                          +--------+
           I
           I
           I
           I
           I
           I
           I
           I
           I
           I    17    45    4    0%
           I******************************************************************
           ILANDSCAPE SITE
           I
           I
           I
           I    23    30   19    0%
           I******************************************************************
           IINSTALL PLUMBING
           I
           I
           I
           I    24    26   23    0%
           I******************************************************************
           IINSTALL GAS
           I
           I
           I
           I    22    20   29    0%
           I******************************************************************
            INSTALL WIRING



            11    64   70    0%
**********************************************************************************
            CONSTRUCT ACCESS ROADS
```

```
+--------+                                  +--------+                                         +--------+
I    140I                                   I    150I                                          I    160I
I11/18/82I      21     32     0    0%  I 1/ 3/83I      25      1     0    0%     I 1/ 4/83I
I11/18/82I*I++++++++++++++++++++++I*I 1/ 3/83I*#+++++++++++++++++++++#*I 1/ 4/83I
I    0   I IINSTALL FITTINGS        I  I    0   I  INAUGURATE BUILDING     IE    0   I
+--------+ I                        I  I +--------+                              +--------+
           I                        I  I
           I                        I  I
           I                        I  I
           I   20     18    14   0%I
           I********************I
              DECORATE INTERIOR   I
                                  I
                                  I
                                  I
                                  I
              17     45     4   0%I
***********************************I
              LANDSCAPE SITE      I
                                  I
                                  I
                                  I
                                  I
              23     30    19   0%I
***********************************I
              INSTALL PLUMBING    I
                                  I
                                  I
                                  I
                                  I
              24     26    23   0%I
***********************************I
              INSTALL GAS         I
                                  I
                                  I
                                  I
                                  I
              22     20    29   0%I
***********************************I
              INSTALL WIRING      I
                                  I
                                  I
                                  I
                                  I
              11     64    70   0%I
***********************************I
              CONSTRUCT ACCESS ROA
```

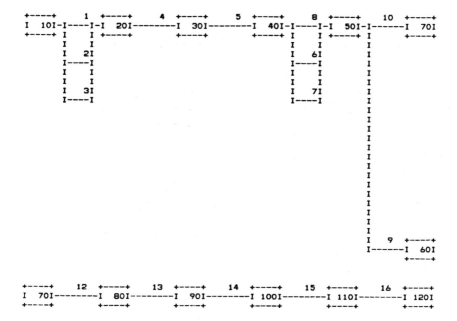

```
+----+      1  +----+      4 +----+      5 +----+      8 +----+     10 +----+
I  10I-I----I-I  20I--------I  30I--------I  40I-I----I-I  50I-I------I  70I
+----+ I    I +----+        +----+        +----+ I    I +----+ I        +----+
       I    I                             I    I         I
       I  2I                              I  6I          I
       I----I                             I----I         I
       I    I                             I    I         I
       I    I                             I    I         I
       I  3I                              I  7I          I
       I----I                             I----I         I
                                                         I
                                                         I
                                                         I
                                                         I
                                                         I
                                                         I
                                                         I
                                                         I
                                                         I
                                                         I
                                                         I
                                                         I  9 +----+
                                                         I------I  60I
                                                           +----+

+----+     12 +----+     13 +----+     14 +----+     15 +----+     16 +----+
I  70I--------I  80I--------I  90I--------I 100I--------I 110I--------I 120I
+----+        +----+        +----+        +----+        +----+        +----+




+----+     11
I  60I----------------------------------------------------------------------
+----+
```

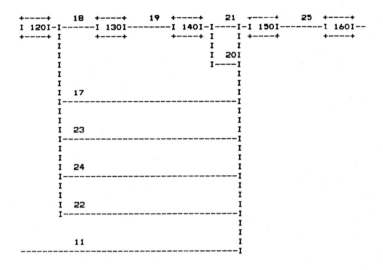

INDEX